MAKING FOR P[

Patterns in Education

Anthony Weaver

BRENTHAM PRESS

First published 1988 by
Brentham Press, 40 Oswald Road, St Albans, Herts AL1 3AQ

ISBN 0 905772 21 0

© Anthony Weaver 1988

Manufacture in UK co-ordinated by Scriptmate, London NW3
6NG

For
RUBY
BEATRICE
CHARLIE
and
THEODORE

CONTENTS

ACKNOWLEDGEMENTS

I wish to thank a number of persons who have given specific encouragement over the writing of this book, all of whom have kindly read and discussed parts or the whole of the manuscript.

The first group comprises friends made through the World Education Fellowship, a body which has taken me to the continent of Europe and to India, Japan, Australia and the United States. Pre-eminent was Jim Henderson, its chairman during my editorship of *The New Era* and whose wisdom was tempered with an unfailing sympathy. Jim Collinge, with whom I have conversed in the southern hemisphere as well as during his study periods in London, has been a scrupulous correspondent from New Zealand. Peter van Stapele and his remarkable family make reciprocal visits between our homes in London and The Hague, and I have been privileged to sit in on his seminars at the University of Leiden.

Peter Cadogan, a former teacher, has been a fearless and prophetic member of the peace movement east and west since our days together in the early 1960s in the Committee of 100. To him, I am indebted for constant stimulation and for his generosity in providing sources on ecology.

On the Peace Education Project of the Peace Pledge Union, Richard Yarwood, a perfect colleague, has illuminated the practicalities in teaching for and about peace. Mildred Masheder and Barbara Winrow have offered discerning suggestions at several stages.

On the organisational side, I could not have been blessed with a more meticulous publisher-and-editor than Margaret Tims of the Brentham Press. I have greatly appreciated the expertise and support of Ann Kritzinger at Scriptmate. Davine Thaw, from South Africa, has been an indefatigable typist and consultant.

Finally, I have enjoyed the hospitality and expert services

of the libraries of the Graduate School of Education at Harvard; of the university at Cambridge, England; and, thanks to Hans Brill, of the Royal College of Art, London.

Anthony Weaver
London, December 1987

FOREWORD

'Only connect' urged E.M. Forster and this is precisely what the author of this book has done. For in it he demonstrates the connection between aesthetic experience, social behaviour and educational method. From his treatment of this theme we can begin to see how, if these three stand in false relationship to one another, what is produced is violence rather than nonviolence, war rather than peace. He has helped me to order my thinking about the future of education by providing me with all kinds of stimulating ideas and references, scattered over eleven at first sight only loosely connected chapters. By using this foreword to describe the focus into which they were brought by my reading of them, I hope to encourage others to achieve a similar result for themselves.

Because education is more determined than determining, it is prudent to begin by identifying those three great laws of human survival, obedience to which is demanded by the present stage of evolution. The first of these laws runs as follows: true patriotism as contrasted with archaic jingoism requires the establishment of limits on the absolute sovereignty of the nation state. The second is that worldwide priority of wealth and endeavour should be devoted to the treatment of the world's food, population and ecology problems as over against expenditure on war or the preparation for it. Man must learn in fact to operate in what Fanon has tellingly described as 'the milieu of scarcity'. 'Bread for myself is a material question: bread for my neighbour is a spiritual one.' (Berdyaev) The third law, by the observance of which the first two can alone be successful, runs to the effect that, as a species and not as fragmented particles called British or Russians, Americans or Chinese, we must recognise and learn to abide by the values which indeed we do have in common. This means the Self as contrasted with the Ego of each one of us, i.e. the midpoint of individual personality, which is the only power capable of transcending and thus redeeming the previously unredeemed egocentrism of man—mutuality in fact as the necessary condition of morality.

The relentless operation of these three laws is what is meant by the strength of the social structure of knowledge. The nature of our informational intake greatly influences our attitudinal reaction to experience. Selected facts (political-economic-psychological) produce conditioned responses. Further, and this is a fact which Weaver's book strongly underpins, what is crucially important for each one of us as we grow from childhood towards maturity is to learn to distinguish between our individual mothers and fathers, lovers, groups and gods and the archetypal images of each of them. The first are multitudinous, different and variable, the second constant and unchanging, while both present themselves to us in their negative as well as positive aspects. For example, there is 'My Mum'—madonna, witch; there's 'My Dad'—good shepherd or brutal bully; there's 'My girl/boy-friend'—Romeo and Juliet or Heathcliff and Catherine; there's 'my enemy'—deadly opponent or necessary foe; there's God or Satan. And the less conscious we are of these powerful images at work in and on our psyches, the more we project them on to the other side (race or class, sex or nation) and so unwittingly enslave ourselves to them.

At the end of his essay on The Will to Believe, William James poses the problem to the solution of which the following pages make a significant contribution:

What do you think of yourself? What do you think of the world? These are riddles of the Sphinx, and in some way or other we must deal with them. If we decide to leave the riddles unanswered, that is a choice, but whatever choice we make, it is at our peril. We stand on a mountain pass in the midst of whirling snow and blinding mist, through which we get glimpses now and then of paths which may prove deceptive. If we stand still, we shall be frozen to death. If we take the wrong road, we shall be dashed to pieces. We do not certainly know there is any right one.

The strength of Anthony Weaver's book is that it does not allow the reader to stand still.

James L Henderson
London, November 1985

1. INTRODUCTION

Faced with the task of bringing up one's own or other people's children, although almost anybody can have a baby in about the time it takes to grow a beard, one is assailed by questions, however exuberantly or light-heartedly the birth was entered upon.

Many parents enjoy the hurly-burly of family life, as well as the binding effect of their joint responsibility. A person's sense of fulfilment and identity tends to be strengthened by having a child, as much as the child's is by the support of his or her parents. This is apart from the desire of some people to produce an heir, or to provide for companionship and support in old age, which may in the event become tyrannical one way or the other.

No doubt the best parents, at any rate of young children, are to be found among those in good health who start their families in a spirit of adventure, content to let the future look after itself. Too much reading of psychology may diminish sponteneity as well as induce feelings of guilt or inadequacy.

However much people accept the conditions in their corner of the world, they must still consider how best to bring up a child, whether he or she be their own progeny or their pupil.

Many would reply that their aim will be to make the child happy. This may be the best answer because it is simple and so much flows from it. 'The true object of education', said William Godwin, in the first sentence of *The Enquirer* (1797) 'like that of every other moral process, is the generation of happiness'. And he added, 'In society the interests of individuals are intertwisted with each other and cannot be separated. Men should be taught to assist each other.'

This quotation seems to be a good starting point because Godwin does emphasise that education is a moral process. Not only is it concerned with intellectual virtue and the training in skills for a job, but with relationships to others wherever or whatever the background. This is to say that a factor in human happiness is mutual aid whose double aspects are interdependent.

Having a regard for others comprises not only the mechanistic acceptance that honesty is the best policy; but the deepest well-being that derives from friendships, sex and affection, as well as from attitudes of pity or charity.

Happiness also implies freedom from poverty, from chronic mental or physical illness (some degree of disability need not impair happiness and may even enhance it); and the encouragement to develop powers of thinking and feeling to the extent to which one is capable.

As an ideal this strengthens the will to use one's powers in a comradely and co-operative manner, and the ability to act and express oneself imaginatively and intelligently.

Many people deplore the violence which seems to be increasing in the world today, whether carried out by governments in the form of repression at home or fighting abroad on whatever scale and with whatever justification; or carried out by individuals in mugging, petty thefts, rioting, desecration, kidnapping or assassination. What can be done about it?

The Gist of the Argument

It is not claimed that what follows is necessarily original, but where the ideas of others are drawn upon, acknowledged or not, the writer can say that he has made them his own. This is perhaps the next best thing to originality, because it is still authentic and tested by further experience. The method has involved a wealth of references which for the reader's convenience are listed in the bibliography.

In 1925 the Hebrew philosopher Martin Buber (1961) described, at a conference of the World Education Fellowship in Heidelberg, the implications of what he called man's instinct for communion and for origination (or creativity). Our main purpose is to examine these somewhat obscure concepts of belonging and making, to extend their meaning and to see how they are interwoven.

To our aid in this task comes that most seminal writer Herbert Read. He was the present author's friend and mentor who gave meaning to the link, encapsulated in a philosophy of nonviolence, between communion and origination.

In Part I we try to show what are, and have been, the psychological obstacles to the enactment of these ideas of Buber, and, in later parts, ways of overcoming them.

In chapter 2 of this part we call upon the wisdom of two non-Freudians: first Winnicott, who suggests how the mother's playing with her baby can enable him or her to symbolise; thus to tolerate her absence, to deal with sometimes fearful phantasies and to assert him or herself in a creative way which may represent the beginnings of the processes of art. Secondly, Ian Suttie argues that 'aggressive emotion is not an instinct but a product of a particular relationship...which is responsible for the whole competitive, self-seeking, power-extolling character of our civilisation.' He indicates that the taboo on aggression, together with the taboo on tenderness, exemplifies the existence of double attitudes.

In chapter 3 we discuss the varying importance given to the aim of an individual's emotional and social integration into family or working groups, since the time of the Renaissance east and west. This recalls the nice distinction between a person's belongings and what he or she belongs to.

We draw upon Read's legion insights to reveal the limitations in Freud's view that the resolution of the alleged oedipus situation results in the postulation of a necessary dependence on leaders (and fathers' internalised conscience) to hold society together. As an alternative there is the path of art.

In chapter 4 James Collinge provides a lucid review of writings on the community theme—'how to create a fraternity for all seasons, for all people'—and explains that through fellowship we can transcend otherwise illusory demands for liberty.

He refers to two writers who embody continuing themes of this book: Johan Galtung claims that 'education is politics', for 'they are both about how society is and how society should be'. Elsewhere Galtung, deriving much from Gandhi, has formulated the notion of 'structural violence' oppressive in itself, and giving rise to unrest and revolts which turn to overt violence. As we shall see, the notion of structural violence, and of education rooted in politics, is well-nigh incomprehensible, indeed anathema, to critics of peace education, although Plato's treatise, *The Republic*, is set in the framework of his desired political state and ensuing social cohesion.

Paulo Freire, writing from a background in South America, has close affinities with Galtung, and in addressing himself to the problem of transformation of societies is insistent that the oppressed must so raise their consciousness that they are able also to understand and succour those who oppress them.

In Part II we move to the world of school-age children, and make use of practical examples highlighted by the extremes of behaviour of delinquent and maladjusted children. Chapter 5 demonstrates the rationale and actual working of a number of systems of shared responsibility. Under a persuasive discipline, thus fostered, the most antisocial children become co-operative and caring towards their fellows. Retributive punishment is eliminated and in its place various forms of spontaneous reparation bear the function of assuaging guilt and making amends.

In complement, chapter 6 shows the therapeutic and intrinsic value of creative activities in personality development. It is hazarded that through such activities the normal academic subjects of the curriculum are illuminated, inspired and linked together. A remarkable protagonist was George Lyward who ran a residential 'place of leisure' for young men. He stimulated music, drama, crafts and his own interests in literature. Moreover his therapy was rooted in the twin notions of love and truth. 'Stern love' he called it, and truth entailed a clear appraisal of current and past relationships in order to understand the origins of the problems. Lyward's embodiment of love and truth had to be earned through his own pain of growing. Unwittingly he exemplified the heart of Gandhi's satyagraha: his love included a willingness to suffer—indeed a kind of reparation, little understood in the Western world.

In Part III we explore the theme of the healing power of art and its explosive nature, which is at once a means by which human beings attain their highest insights and flights of expression, as well as seeming to pose threats to upholders of established order.

Our central theme is firmly based on the belief in the dynamic power of sheer line, colour, form (Kandinsky), and in the reality of the 'aesthetic condition', as expounded by Friedrich Schiller (echoing Plato) which, though in his view of no significance in itself, creates a mood that enables us to attain a moral awareness. 'Man is superior to every terror of Nature', he said, 'as long as he knows how to give form to it, and turn it into his object'.

Several reactions derive from the recognition of the explosive power of art. There have been attempts to use it for religious or political ends such as the procession carrying Duccio's new masterpiece to the duomo in Siena, or Lunarcharsky's exploitation of the theatre in the new Soviet Union. Secondly, there has been an effort to stifle its exuberance, notably under Christian influence (e.g. rarity of the male nude other than the *dead* Christ). There is the somewhat blind wish to categorise art as merely a speeded-up way of thinking; to extol activity, as exemplified by John Dewey and his followers on the Zero project at Harvard, who largely ignore the haptic basis for expression. In opposition to this we record Peter Abbs' illuminating discussion of the effects of Descartes' concept of the self as pure mind 'wholly distinct from the body and even more easily known than the latter'. In this there was no place for the culture of feelings, and least of all a place for wholeness of heart and mind running harmoniously together. Yet Abbs stresses the importance of traditional as well as of innovative culture. Each is needed to inform the other, and the latter to enliven what may otherwise become a static and coercive community.

In Part IV we attempt to draw threads together. Chapter 9 on the one hand traces the historical precedents and psychological mechanisms which perpetuate the idea of the virile hero, destined to die a glorious death in battle; and the all too common need to have an enemy. On the other hand, it outlines a feasible world in which, suicidal weapons having been abandoned, poverty and discrimination are eliminated. This entails a recognition of the constants and variables between the ways of life of the peoples of the world, and a leap in human habit to change to nonviolent forms for the non-provocative defence and promotion of cultural freedom and economic well-being.

In Chapter 10, starting with John Evelyn in the seventeenth century, we briefly trace ecological and caring reactions to the ruthless exploitation of the finite resources of the planet—accelerated it seems by the inventions of gunpowder, the compass and the printing press. Peter Kropotkin is held as a key late nineteenth century figure whose researches into the organisation of animal life led him to establish the nature, and indeed the necessity, of mutual aid (in contrast to Darwin) in place of competition, for the benefit of the inhabitants of the globe.

It is strongly suggested that modern technology has come to the aid of political decentralisation. Among the latest influential exponents of the evils of over-industrialisation and of pollution have been the Friends of the Earth and the Green Parties in Germany, US, and the UK. In association with some aspects of the women's peace movement, they have established distinctions between work and employment (ie. the gift economy). And they are in line with those who see a fatal connection between the militarisation of society and adherence to outmoded forms of industrial sovereignty.

Incidentally, but not accidentally, it is argued that small-scale self-sufficiency provides the underpinning for an organisation of the world in regional, polycentric confederations.

In conclusion, in chapter 11, mindful of the springs of human motivation and aspiration, we affirm that education has always emanated from a social and moral basis. Since 1945 the latter has had urgently to encompass education for peace. Bringing in a new dimension upsets the upholders of traditional curriculum; bringing in an awareness of the predicaments of the nuclear age disturbs the political assumptions and mores of our time. Hence it engenders opposition.

Three main considerations are suggested: that learning to practise better forms of conflict resolution lies at the heart of the matter, that conflict itself is welcomed as a stimulus for change. Secondly, that indoctrination is no more entailed, nor to be feared, than in other subjects such as religious studies, history or biology. Though teachers may, and should, hold strong convictions their businees is to differentiate between conscious viewpoint and unconscious bias in themselves and in their pupils. Thirdly, that education, and hence peace studies, are fields of knowledge (comparable say to geography or engineering) which are not academic disciplines in themselves, but which draw upon distinctive methods, notably, in the case of education, of psychology, history and philosophy.

Part I

INGREDIENTS OF A SUPPORTING COMMUNITY

2. EMOTIONAL BONDS AND AGGRESSION

Emotional Bonds and the Infant's Trust
Aggression and Guilt

We now attempt to look at the somewhat haphazard way in which children are brought into the world, some motives of parents and the actual processes and constant qualities that should enter into early education.

Emotional Bonds and the Infant's Trust

Winnicott (1958) used to say that there is no such thing as a baby, but only a baby-and-its-mother. To this important observation we might add that 'mother' here means the woman or man, whether biological parent or not, who consistently looks after the child day after day during the first six to twelve months of its life, whether or not breast-fed initially. From this context, it is a vital step to consider what other persons can have a significant influence upon the baby's early character development.

The human infant's comparatively long physical dependence, in contrast to other mammals or chicks or whatever, seems to suggest that his or her immaturity has several functions—namely, to provide time and opportunity for subtle emotional development in itself, and a basis upon which later social and intellectual (and indeed physical) development depend. The main function of the period of dependence, however, is to provide an arena for the process of conscious differentiation without too much anxiety. How is this?

Somehow human beings have survived the trauma of each one's birth, somehow parents have been good enough for that. But there are and have been great disparities, just as there are and have been avoidable famines amongst plenty, tyrannies and exploitation by one group of people over another.

Initially part of, and wholly dependent upon, his or her mother, the baby gradually discovers that they are physically separate. The baby wants the breast, we are told, at every whim, for food, and perhaps of more importance, for comfort and reassurance. The great lesson for the baby to learn is that despite his or her frustration and ensuing despair, mother will return and has not been annihilated by her baby's anger. In healthy conditions this experience leads to the assurance that both can survive the hazards of mother's departures and baby's retaliatory hatred.

Where the mother, for reasons no doubt to be found in her own life story, cannot bring herself to be consistent, or abhors a fondling relationship, the poor baby will remain unintegrated, or in Dockar Drysdale's terms (1968), pre-neurotic. A less severe detriment to character seems to account for a major origin of neurosis, or inbuilt anxiety, where the baby has integrated but is treated to too pro-longed and haphazard periods of rejection or separation.

Surviving the hazards, however, is concomitant with growth. Successful experience here may begin to set a pat-tern for accepting difficulties and problems as opportu-nities. A healthy baby will feel the first twinges of guilt that he or she has mistrusted the mother, maybe hurt her by biting, and feel wretched and somehow to blame for having brought about her disregard or even hatred and rejection. One reaction to guilt is aggression, but another is to make amends. If the mother has the love, strength and patience she will promote in the baby some acts of reparation, which may amount to no more than *feelings* of forgiveness, as a result of which she will find herself unscathed.

A happy outcome to the baby's inevitable frustration forms a strong basis for tolerance in later life. By the nature of things the mother cannot always be available: she has other interests, responsibilities and demands upon her time and energy. She and her baby can learn to understand that this fact of life means no lack of love between them, and nor is the loss primarily caused by the father. He, in some partnerships, shares in providing, or may provide all the care other than actual breast feeding. When things have gone wrong, when the baby's fear and aggression seek a scapegoat, then there may be a projection of blame for loss of mother's attention on to the father. Only then may an oedipus complex develop, and even that can be assuaged not simply by internalising the father's forbidding attitudes in the form of conscience, or super ego, but once again through symbolic acts of reparation.

At an early vital stage, before talking, mother and father and baby play together. Related to thumb sucking, which can be a help in weaning, how often do we see a small child carrying about, sucking, and clinging to an old rag or part of a soft toy? The rag is not merely a comforter or soother, though it is that, but seems to stand symbolically between the thumb which is part of the child, and an external object, which he or she is able to recognise. It can represent phantasies, which can be played with pleasurably and in fear. Above all, this thing can symbolise mother, her breast, the loved one. It can help the child to deal with the inevitable maternal failure, since she cannot completely adapt to the baby's needs. Winnicott (1974), with great insight, has developed the notion of this thing as a 'transitional object' or transitional phenomenon. In too prolonged absence of the mother, the 'transitional object' loses its meaning for the child who cannot sustain the phantasy. Or if the thing is disregarded, swept away, ridiculed or lost, the grounding of his or her powers of imagination may be stunted or shattered. Having provided the illusion of her eternal presence through responding to the baby's demands, the mother creates an arena by playing together, in which her child can learn to cope through creative experience with the essential disillusionment. The baby must learn that he or she is not able, omnipotently like Aladdin with his lamp, to summon her at will. Separation from mother can be endured as the baby learns in her presence to fill it in through symbolic play.

Aggression and Guilt

In the adult world today aggression is condemned, both on the national and personal level, but it is also admired as a sign of virility and courage—and war is extolled as a means of promoting such attributes. The double-think about aggression, however, is partly explained semantically. First, in the popular sense, it means a move with the intention to hurt or destroy. Secondly, in the clinical sense, self-assertion (or, in the infant, motility) is taken to refer strictly to the expression of energy, comparable to Shaw's life-force or Adler's striving, which though unwittingly causing harm or damage, has not this intention. In this book 'aggression' will be used in the popular sense; 'self-assertion' in the clinical.

A further confusion arises over whether aggression, in the popular sense, is innate, that is to say in varying degrees, inherited.

Suttie (1935, p.62), and later Jackson (1954), came to the conclusion that the initial emotions of the human infant are those of dependence and need for love, by which security is ensured. Only when the demand for love is frustrated (and this may be inevitable) does revengeful behaviour arise. 'The refusal of the mother to give to the child leads to anxiety, hate, aggression and to the quest for power. Aggressive emotion is not an instinct but a product of a particular relationship to environment.' (1935, p.62) In Suttie's view this particular relationship is responsible for 'the whole competitive, self-seeking, power extolling character of our civilisation'. (op. cit., ch 6). And he suggested that the taboo on aggression, as well as the taboo on tenderness, exemplifies the existence of double attitudes to both.

It is appropriate to consider again the work of Winnicott on the origins of aggression, for not only does he implicitly acknowledge the work of Freud and Adler (1921), and appears to have built upon that of Anna Freud (1937), Klein (1937), Bovet (1957) and Himmelweit (1950), but he inspired much of the practice of Dockar Drysdale (1963, 1968).

Winnicott postulated that the infant's motility, as an expression of life-force, is in existence even during the foetal stage. Owing to its motility the growing embryo discovers the opposition of the environment in the form of mother's body, and after the birth is eventually led to the concept of 'me' and 'not-me'. Contact with other persons enables the baby to feel real, leaving aside for the moment the meaning of this contact, that is to say whether it is positive or negative.

A baby kicks in the womb; it cannot be assumed that it is trying to kick its way out. A baby of a few weeks thrashes away with his arms; it cannot be assumed that he means to hit. A baby chews the nipple with his gums; it cannot be assumed that he is meaning to destroy or hurt. (1958, p.204)

Hence, the action is not aggressive in the popular sense. The baby does not appreciate that what it hurts when excited is the same as that which it values in quiet intervals between excitements. Excited love includes attacks on mother's body. If the baby did not (unwittingly) hurt the mother he or she would lose to some degree the capacity to love, that is to say, to make relationships.

Hence there comes into being a feeling of grief and of guilt. The guilt refers to the damage which is felt to be done to the loved person. In health the infant can hold the guilt and, with help, discover his or her own personal urge 'to give and to construct and to mend'.

Through playing he or she learns that the expression of frustrated feelings will not destroy the parent. If it were not for motility, the development of reciprocal feelings and awareness could not take place. Through their understanding of the total situation, father and mother are not in fact hurt—a point full of meaning for adult relationships. In times of helplessness (as when no person can be found to accept a gift or to acknowledge effort to repair) this transformation breaks down and aggression or revenge appear.

Freud, it would seem, did not go far enough in his childhood studies. The result was that since his patients explained to him that aggressive experiences were the ones that made them feel most real, he concluded that aggression, as an intention to hurt, was a fundamental wish. He did not see that aggression is a contradiction in terms at the earliest stages, and that it is later resorted to by people who have been deprived of, or who have lost, the means of transformation of guilt. It is as though Freud had examined numbers of under-nourished people and concluded that their physiognomy was unalterable and typical of mankind.

Freud's assumption that aggression, as distinct from self-assertion, is part of the ineradicable animal nature of human beings, seems to have little evidence to support it. When aggression does arise, induced no doubt historically in acquisitive and competitive societies, it tends to look for, and to fix upon, some external object, and perhaps derive sadistic pleasure from so doing. It may of course be sublimated, such as in the activities of a surgeon, in a way that is socially useful and approved of.

On the other hand it may turn itself inward as self-aggression, and, though perhaps deriving masochistic pleasure from that, give rise to psychosomatic symptoms.

To postulate aggression as an inevitable human trait, whether directed outwardly or inwardly, appears to ignore the psychological reactions expounded by Suttie, and the significance of creative processes as a means of transformation.

3. THE NOTION OF AN INDIVIDUAL

It is all too common to say that we value a person as an individual and to assume that the task of education is to help him or her to become one more fully.

In the western world the Renaissance above all meant a return to the Hellenic valuation of the intellect and of a person's individuality. In praise of his fellow Athenians Pericles proclaims in his funeral oration 'For we have a peculiar power of thinking and of acting too, whereas other men are courageous from ignorance but hesitate upon reflection.'

This ideal would seem to have been shared by Buddha, but was in contrast to Hebrew traditions, to Christian tenets so far as the original sin was to taste the fruit of the tree of knowledge, and certainly in contrast to the submission demanded of followers of Islam.

Such an ideal has run like a thread through the previous chapter: but it needs qualifying.

No-one can have read Huizinga (1937), the Dutch historian, without feeling some doubt about what date to ascribe to the beginning of the Renaissance and about the nature of its origins. Nevertheless, the previous period was dominated by notions of hierarchy (or dharma in Hindu philosophy) and chivalry, the latter deriving, via the Romans, from Homer's epic stories which extolled the honour and glory of a noble death in battle. Such glory, according to Burckhardt (1944), took a collective form, and indeed the codes of chivalry, as of painting, depended for their merit on meticulous adherence to precedent.

At the universities, scholastic texts were held to contain the wisdom of ages and were there to be learnt, studied and combed through over and over again. In parallel, innovatory hypotheses, or discoveries of scientists, such as Galileo, were condemned because they challenged the tenets of received Christianity.

'All terrestrial beauty', writes Huizinga, (1937, p.30), 'bore the stain of sin. Even where art and piety succeeded in hallowing it by placing it in the service of religion, the artist or the lover of art had to take care not to surrender to the charms of colour and line. All noble life was in its essential manifestations full of such beauty tainted by sin.'

One has only to see the exuberance in animal forms of the Pompeii frescoes in the first century A.D. to be aware of the subsequent inhibiting impact of Christianity (for its own reasons) on the powers of artistic expression. By the sixteenth century it was the very *spontaneity* of expression that marked out the modern masters.

In our own day it is easy enough to criticise the exigencies of a regime such as the Soviet Union which, as Plato urged for his *Republic*, puts a curb on freedom for every person, not only for the artist, who might undermine the stability of the State.

To be compared in this context are the differing aims of psychoanalysis in Japan and the United States, which in fact reveal quite different standards in an assessment of mental health.

Barbara Wootton (1959, p.218) made a thorough study of this and related matters. She writes:

In the literature of mental health generally, (the) concept of adjustment is particularly prominent. Fine phrases cannot, however, obscure the fact that adjustment means adjustment to a particular culture or to a particular set of institutions; and that to conceive adjustment and maladjustment in medical terms is in effect to identify health with the ability to come to terms with that culture or with those institutions—be they totalitarian methods of government, the dingy culture of an urban slum, the contemporary English law of marriage or...the standards of an acquisitive, competitive, hierarchical, envious society.

In the application of their techniques to cultures other than their own, psychiatrists and other experts in mental hygiene often show themselves to be alive to the presence of this slippery element in their own definitions. Thus Moloney (1954) describes how the authoritarian mores of the Japanese conflict with the psychoanalytic aim of creating free, adaptable individuals. The aim of therapy in psychiatric as distinct from psychoanalytic practice should, he thinks, be frankly to adjust the patient to the demands of his society; but for the psychoanalyst, the answer to the question 'to be or not to be free?' he finds more difficult. 'Should the American and the Japanese psychoanalytic therapist', he asks, 'encourage individualism or should they insist upon insensible and unconscious submissive conformity to the existing culture?' The Japanese psychoanalyst, faced with the problem of curing a mentally ill person, must first of all diagnose him as 'ill' because he does not adhere to rigidly prescribed culture patterns...The 'cure' upon which the analyst then embarks constitutes the opposite of a cure by western standards. Instead of endeavouring, as do occidental psychoanalysts, to free the individual from his inner thongs, the Japanese analyst actually tightens those thongs.

There is however a possible positive side to the characteristics of a collective, to be seen in China or the early kibbutzim in Israel which knowingly, for good or bad, induce a co-operative style of individuality. The following paraphrase of an article by Stephen Coates (1962, pp.935-37) is significant and contains affinities with, and divergencies from, Sigmund Freud.

Conscience is the inheritor of our childhood loves. We loved our parents, and from the image we formed of them grew our own inner image of good and bad, true and untrue. From their individual personalities we formed our own individual personalities. As they were the products of a particular society, in time and place, so, through our identification with them, we became inheritors of the values of that society. Through our love for our parents, and other loved educators, the values of society are handed down to us. The nature and extent of our altruism, our morality and ethics are very much determined by the type of family in which we grew up (e.g. Arapesh and Mundugumor). It would follow that different kinds of families will produce different kinds of consciences. And it may be useful to ask whether the family structure of Western society is likely to produce a conscience which is altruistic and creative.

The problem is whom can we love, or whom may we love? By living under only one father, with only our real brothers and sisters, do we thus restrict our capacity to extend our love and concern to people outside that immediate world? It is remarkable how much is done gratuitously within the family and how little is done gratuitously outside it.

Do we create too narrow and individual a conscience, concerned too much with inner guilt, too little with the needs of the group? Perhaps the strain of an individual conscience is too great?

By some standards the kibbutz children are deprived. But they do not seem to be delinquent, rather they seem to be identified with a larger group than the individual family. In such a group it may be that loves are weaker, individual ties are weaker: but equally hates will be weaker. The identification from which the conscience arises will be not only with *one loved,* and hated, parent, but with many loved and hated adults. Such a conscience may be weaker, less likely to produce neurosis, which is the product of an over rigid unconscious conscience: and being weaker, control of the personality may be less in the conscience than in the conscious parts of the mind. Then recognising, from the whole of his childhood experience, the interdependence of each upon each, the man may more rationally choose co-operation in place of competition: altruism in place of destruction.

The crucial questions that Coates asks are with what person or group are human beings capable of identifying and by what processes are they brought to do so?

He and other writers (e.g. Bettelheim, 1969) have shown that in adult life kibbutzniks' loyalties, owing to their early upbringing by the metapale rather than exclusively by their own parents from the first day of life, are more diffused than children reared in the nuclear family. Whether for necessity in an economy of scarcity or whether for the sake of an ideal, the Israelis undoubtedly launched into these practices (later somewhat modified) with their eyes open—to the plentiful translations in Hebrew of the works of John Bowlby (1946, 1951).

It will have been noticed that Coates attributes the formation of conscience in Freudian manner to the internalising of the infant's authorities. He does not here refer to the super-ego and he assumes that 'parents', not solely the father, can provide the model. From this stance, of course, it is easier, as in fact happens, to expand from 'the parents' to a larger group of adults.

At this point, whatever view one may take of the theology of id, ego and super-ego, it would be as well to make two quotations from Freud himself (1923, pp.34-5):

The child's parents, and especially his father, were perceived as the obstacle to a realisation of his oedipus wishes; so his infantile ego fortified itself for the carrying out of the repression by erecting this same obstacle within itself. It borrowed strength to do this, so to speak, from the father, and this loan was an extraordinarily momentous act. The super-ego retains the character of the father, while the more powerful the oedipus complex was, and the more rapidly it succumbed to repression (under the influence of authority, religious teaching, schooling and reading), the stricter will be the domination of the super-ego over the ego later on—in the form of conscience or perhaps of an unconscious sense of guilt.

So it is postulated that the new oedipal identification contains the power of the authoritative father, which lies in the special characteristic of the super-ego. It may be that when he wrote this Freud was already doubting whether the same would be true for the feminine oedipus complex in reverse. Though elsewhere he tentatively substitutes 'parents' for father, in line with Stephen Coates on the kibbutzim, ultimately he insists that it is the father, and not the two parents, who plays this repressive role.

In developing his notion of inheritance, Freud comes near to that of Jung's collective unconscious, except for the introduction of the super-ego.

He continues:

The experiences of the ego seem at first to be lost for inheritance; but when they have been repeated often enough and with sufficient strength in many individuals in successive generations, they transform themselves, so to say, into experiences of the id, the impressions of which are preserved by heredity. Thus in the id, which is capable of being inherited, are harboured residues of the existences of countless egos; and, when the ego forms its super-ego out of the id, it may perhaps only be reviving shapes of former egos and be bringing them to resurrection.

In a nutshell here we have a statement of Freudian theory that it is from the *father* that conscience is derived, and that through the formation of super-ego the boy inherits his social sense, religion, and culture.

Upon this premise, psychoanalytical theory has been logically, though somewhat mechanistically, developed, and most eloquently expressed. Human beings the world over are indebted to Freud's observations and tireless work. But to the present writer, as well as to certain feminists, it is too clever by half, and provides an illusory prop to the notion of paternalism.

An extremely thorough and illuminating exposition has been provided by Juliet Mitchell (1974). A mine of information, she critically discusses the work of Reich, Laing, de Beauvoir, Friedan, Figes, Greer, Firestone and Millett to show how they diverge from Freud's line. In doing so, in the present writer's view, she reveals herself entrapped in a straitjacket of patriarchy, as an inevitable feature of human society hitherto, from which the only escape will come through the bizarre contradictions of the nuclear family. 'It is *fathers* not men', she says, 'who have the determinate power'.

What happens to the oedipus theory in societies where the father is not known and the maternal uncle plays a dominant role? As mentioned above we do know something from the experience of the kibbutzim of the different character formation that occurs when the father *is* known, but, with the mother, plays only a subsidiary role.

As already pointed out it is not just 'jealous father', but the demands of her other children and her own intrinsic interests, that makes the mother not available all the time to her youngest baby.

Some critics of Freud have been unable to accept the oedipus theory, on the grounds that it cannot be universal for it does not apply to girls in the same way and that the Elektra story is a poor substitute. Such critics have ignored Freud's very own explanation that it is precisely because of this that he opposed any idea of symmetry in the cultural making of men and women. That the oedipus complex does not apply to girls shows, in Freud's view, that their superegos are weaker. They are not themselves heirs to the law of the father and are thus compelled to enter a man's world on his terms. This is supposed to have been the case in all human civilisations. How then do women come by their conscience and sense of justice?

A further question on the sources of morality, as hazarded by Freud, is tied up with his view of identification with, and indeed the necessity for, a leader. He wrote (1940, p.70):

A path leads by way of imitation to empathy, that is, to the comprehension of the mechanism by means of which we are enabled to take up any attitude at all towards another mental life. Moreover, there is still much to be explained in the manifestations of existing identifications. These result among other things in a person limiting his aggressiveness towards those with whom he has identified himself ...

And he also says (op. cit., pp. 65-66):

We already begin to divine that the mutual tie between the members of a group is in the nature of an identification...and we may suspect that this common quality lies in the nature of the tie with the leader. Another suspicion may tell us that we are far from having exhausted the problem of identification, and that we are faced by the process which psychology calls 'empathy'...But we shall here limit ourselves to the immediate emotional effects of identification, and shall leave to one side its significance for our intellectual life.

Perhaps we *should* examine the significance, and the means, of identification in our intellectual life. When Freud said that a path leads by way of imitation to empathy he may or may not have been referring to the path of art.

Of course, there is the path of identification with the leader which can easily lead to an authoritarian relationship, or even a totalitarian one, in which no empathy is involved.

Herbert Read (1970, p.142) commented on this passage of Freud, and, as Collinge points out in Chapter 4, championed the close link between art and morality; that morality has an aesthetic basis, not primarily a legal or religious or social/psycholigical one—though these influences are of course involved. Read said:

Morality is essentially mutuality—the sharing of a common ideal. And the process by which we are induced to share a common ideal is...by the creation of an empathic relationship with our fellows...by means of common rituals, by means of the imitation of the same patterns—by meeting as it were in the common form or quality of the universally valid work of art...

From the psychological point of view, the social function of art takes on an additional importance; it saves us from identification with a leader—it excludes the tyranny of the person; it unites us in the impersonal beauty of art.

We hope to show in the course of this book that an oedipus complex, if it does arise, can be assuaged through play, and that dependence upon leaders is by no means the only way for society to ensure its stability.

4. COMMUNITY AND EDUCATION:
Some Recent Writings

This survey, by James Collinge of the University of Wellington, New Zealand, draws together strands on the community theme. It is suggested that through fellowship we can transcend what are otherwise illusory demands for liberty.

In the trenches of the First World War, Herbert Read experienced a kind of interpersonal cohesion among the men that was the embodiment of his social ideal. It was, he wrote (1968, p.41), the fidelity of one man to another, in circumstances of common danger, the fidelity of all men in a group to one another and to the group as a whole.

This unity, which Read called 'morale', arose spontaneously out of the social activities of people living in a community with mutual aid as its inspiring purpose. He hoped that the comradeship that had developed between the soldiers would lead to a new social order when peace came, but, of course, the spirit disappeared with the removal of the common danger, the only new quality being that of exhaustion.

The problem with which this chapter is largely concerned is how to create in society a cohesiveness between individuals that is both natural and permanent but not reliant upon external forces or strong leadership from above. It is a subject in which education has a central role and on which a number of writers in recent years have made important statements. Some of them will be briefly reviewed here. Out of this review some principles will be drawn defining the nature of community and its educational implications.

For Read, the solution lay largely in an education that was both moral and aesthetic. Aesthetic education properly conceived was also moral education and as such the basis of a true community. Morale was to be achieved by a kind of conditioning process in which the mind of the child could be developed into patterns of thought and behaviour which were beautiful, which accorded with the physical patterns found in the objective world, in the formal structure of organic and inorganic phenomena. Through the experience of art children would exemplify in their own persons grace, rhythm and harmony, they would grow into people who would act and think according to aesthetic criteria and thus be more likely, Read believed, to exhibit the social unity and cohesiveness that is the end result of moral education. 'Aesthetic education develops ethical virtue'. (1970, p.218)

Art then must be a universal experience for all people, not left to a special few in a great metropolis. It grew out of the soil, out of the people, out of their daily life and work. A true artistic culture for Read was the spontaneous expression of a people's joy in life and work. If this joy did not exist, culture did not exist. Read thought that he had found something approaching this ideal in the People's Republic of China. Here was a society, with vast industrial and technical expertise, which had managed to decentralise to the extent that its populace still lived in communities that were in a real sense organic. He saw poems written by peasants pinned up on the notice-board in the village hall, undoubtedly not very good poems, but, as he wrote (1968, p.59), millions of them are written among the pigs and the water-buffaloes and from such a ferment an essence will remain.

The same concern with local roots has recently been expressed by Ivan Illich (1981), who contends that vernacular values, the people's culture, are constantly being threatened by powerful centralising forces in the modern world. Illich points out that vast resources are expended through compulsory education to create a standard culture and a standardised language; schools are places where people learn to speak as they should, and in the process local languages are degraded.

The colonisation of language is, for Illich, a crucial factor in a wider civil war against popular and traditional cultures. Through untutored language a sense of power within the group exists; language that is purposefully taught destroys the sense of cohesion in a traditional community. This process is but an aspect of a commodity-intensive society in which work is defined as paid employment and where most traditional work is relegated to a second 'shadow' economy of unpaid work, necessary for the continuation of the industrial economy, but essentially unrecognised. This creates a form of apartheid, with a class of victims who do the dirty work and who, if they are considered at all, are the objects of sentimental compassion.

Hostile critics of Illich might accuse him of being simplistic, of being a dewy-eyed unrealistic romantic, unable to see the real privations of traditional cultures in which people live Hobbsean lives, 'solitary, poor, nasty, brutish and short'. Be that as it may, one does not have to be too radical a feminist to see the force of Illich's argument that the modern economy has created a sexual apartheid in which the housewife is an icon of a shadow existence, concerned with unpaid work off the job, demanding no special qualifications, not regarded as productive and therefore given no social prestige. And most Third World countries provide plentiful examples of the results of the destruction of local culture and technology: rural poverty and stagnation, urban unemployment and overcrowding, growing dependence upon rich countries and the exclusion of the mass of the population from the processes of production.

Illich's name is often linked with that of Paulo Freire (1972), an educator whose life's work has been concerned with the oppressed. There are crucial differences between the two, which will be dealt with later, but they are united in their analysis of the ways in which elite groups exercise domination over people who are exploited, denied an effective voice in their own lives and, as a result, are unable to develop a true identity, a consciousness of themselves and their position in the world. Freire's term for this is 'the culture of silence' in which the oppressed view the world by means of powerful and pervasive myths engendered by the oppressors; they see themselves through the oppressors' eyes. The result is an attitude of fatalism, a feeling of worthlessness and self-doubt.

While Freire is writing from a background of experience in the Third World, the same mechanisms can be seen to apply in the West. Our economic system has created a large and increasing class of unemployed people who, far from being shown the true economic basis of unemployment, are encouraged by powerful élite-controlled media to view the problem as being to a large extent their own fault. The 'unemployed' very quickly become 'unemployable', not victims of an unjust economic system but deficient of necessary skills and abilities. They are incapable of seeing the reality of the situation, are 'unable to name the world'.

The traditional Western type education system is regarded by Freire as a social institution that is used by élites to help maintain oppression. They are a powerful element in the process of domestication. Freire's term for the process is 'banking' education. Nevertheless, education also lies at the heart of Freire's solution to the problem, but it is an education for liberation, not one of teacher and taught but of an exploration of the world undertaken by equals, an exploration that results is action which in turn generates further reflection and so on, an education in 'praxis'.

The process of coming, through education, to understand the world and one's position in it is what Freire calls 'conscientizacao'. The word has been somewhat misunderstood in the West, and, as a result, the notion has itself become domesticated. It does not mean, as is sometimes thought, searching totally within oneself for a subjective internal reality. In an interview with Rex Davis (Mackie, 1980), Freire expresses his conviction that people can never liberate themselves alone in their own consciousness. The process of liberation arises in communion, in dialogue, in the relationships between people and the world and a reality which is then transformed. Education is thus a political process which has as its ideal a community of equals engaged in dialogue with a critical awareness of reality and the ability to transform it.

Stig Lindholm (1975) enormously influenced by Freire, has coined the apt term 'moving towards the world' for this process. Through critical awareness humans find themselves faced with reality—with nature, other people, social structures—a reality that defies and provokes them. Lindholm calls this the 'animation' process, a growing consciousness of oneself in a social situation which demands that humans join together to develop both a sense of personal identity and meaning, and an outer involvement in close community.

One problem with this view of human consciousness is that it can be regarded as basically a culturally-specific Western pattern of thinking which is not necessarily appropriate to non-Western cultures. As Bower (1983, pp.935-53) has pointed out, the dominant Western pattern of thinking places a high value on abstract-theoretical thought, which is reproduced by Freire in metaphors like freedom, liberation, critical reflection, praxis and the idea that the historical mission of human beings is to create a new society. Bower contrasts this view with those of the Chipewyan in Alberta, Canada, for whom true knowledge is concrete and pragmatic and for whom abstraction means losing control. The world views of the Chipewyan are thus based on reality assumptions fundamentally different from the Christian, Marxist and existentialist thought of Freire. Bower writes that if Freire were to use his adult literacy programme with the Chipewyan 'he would undoubtedly welcome the opportunity to emancipate another group from the oppression of their own history'.

This form of cultural intervention can thus be seen as another example of the universal education involving a standard language that Illich has shown increases a ruler's control over the people and their local culture. Here there is a fundamental difference between Freire and Illich. Vernacular values which constitute a source of strength within the group are, as Bower has noted, for Freire a hindrance to the growth and planning of the state. Supporters will no doubt object that this is a misreading of Freire, that he is concerned with cohesive communities rather than with the state as the source of total political power. Nevertheless, certain aspects of Freire's more recent work in Guinea-Bissau (Freire, 1978) are more concerned with the development of a nation state according to Government plans, a far cry from the self-sufficient, cohesive community. In fact, as Jim Walker has shown, Freire's emphasis on leadership and the party as a vehicle of the people's expression negates some of his most basic ideals (Mackie, 1980).

There is no space here to discuss further Freire's com-

plex, if somewhat contradictory thought. Two points, however, must be made. Firstly, it may well be that Freire's
pedagogy finds a natural home within a Western cultural
context. It is certainly my experience that Western students
find Freire's ideas extremely exciting but that students from
the Pacific or from South Asia are often much less enthu-
siastic. Secondly, many of the oppressed peoples with whom
Freire is concerned have already been faced with colonial-
ism and industrial power, and it is from this cultural destruction rather than from their traditional world view that
their inability to 'name the world' stems.

One fear that is commonly expressed about the tightly-
knit, cohesive community is that, whatever positive values
it possessed, there would also be a considerable loss of
individuality. It is a commonplace of anarchist thought that
strong methods of control would in a small, non-alienating
community give way to control by pressure of public opinion, praise and blame, which would become a tyranny ultimately more destructive of human liberty and individuality
than government from above.

George Orwell (1968, pp.215-216) was certainly aware of
the power of public opinion. In his discussion of the political significance of *Gulliver's Travels*, he attacked what he
called the 'totalitarian tendency' implicit in communities in
which the only arbiter of behaviour is public opinion.

When human beings are governed by 'thou shalt not', the individual can practise a certain amount of eccentricity: when they are
supposedly governed by 'love' or 'reason', he is under continuous
pressure to make him behave and think in exactly the same way as
everyone else.

Orwell saw a vision of this society in the Houyhnhnms who
never discussed any topics (apart from how to deal with
Yahoos), who never disagreed and who apparently had no
word for opinion in their language.

Perhaps one way out of the dilemma is to emphasise
what Crick has called the 'forgotten value', fraternity. This
involves common tasks and activities, working with other
people towards common ends. Fraternity, says Crick, may
not always involve liberty; it is better if it does, but it does

not mean treating everyone the same. There must be a
recognition of the diversity of character; fraternity 'is concerned with how individuals can contribute best to the
common tasks of reforming society, living in and creating
genuine communities.' (1978, p.150)

Crick is concerned with Read's problem outlined at the
beginning of this chapter: how can we create a fraternity
for all seasons and for all people such as that which
emerges on great occasions of war, emergency and struggle?
It cannot exist in a society of division and class barriers,
but is enhanced by doing things together both in community
relations and in the work place. Crick believes that this task
is possible although he says 'sceptics all too often defend
the rotten competitive values of the present which makes
"success" for some mean failure or deprivation for others'.
(ibid, p.156)

Education systems, however, are not usually concerned
with genuine engagement in common tasks leading to a
genuine sense of community, but often engender instead a
spirit of competitive materialism which inevitably leads to
non-peaceful relationships. Adam Curle has criticised competitive materialistic education systems which are inimical
to the development of true community. In his book *Education for Liberation* (1973) he is concerned to show how
education might, but usually does not, contribute to peaceful relationships. An interesting and refreshing feature of
this book is the honesty with which Curle repudiates his
earlier views on education (*Educational Strategy for Developing Societies*, 1963) in which he argued that the wide
spread of education would help people to become aware of
their oppression due to poverty, class or race, that it would
thus become a force for equality and economic development.
Curle has now become more than a little disillusioned with
this view of education, which he feels promotes competitive
materialism and is dominated by a 'belonging identity'
which leads to 'unpeaceful relationships in which the powerful diminish the potential of the weak'. (ibid p.8)

(However, in a private letter to A. Weaver, 14 October
1987, he explains that by belonging, which he had defined
in *Militants and Mystics*, he intended to refer to the sense

in which we think of ourselves in terms of what we belong *to* 'being part of a loving family or other group...which *does* free us of those neurotic preoccupations'.)

However, the system need not be completely dominant. Curle is of the belief that in both society and human nature there is an equally connected counter-system of higher awareness, based more on altruism than on the self-protective character of competitive materialism. The human relationships are in general peaceful, the institutions are co-operative, egalitarian and democratic. Much of Curle's book is devoted to showing how such a counter-system can be encouraged and developed.

All the writers dealt with so far in this chapter are agreed upon the devastating effect of competitive materialism upon our lives: it engenders divisions of class, sex and race, friction and ultimately war. It creates a permanent class of oppressed and inhibits the awareness of community. The solutions put forward are various. For Read, a true romantic, the source of redemption was art and education through art which unites rather than divides. Illich and his followers advocate the dismantling of the whole educational edifice, to be replaced by a network of voluntary, co-operative relationships, a notion which has been a staple of much anarchist thought ever since Godwin in the eighteenth century. Similarly Freire, while not advocating deschooling necessarily, is adamant that true education is a co-operative venture between teacher and student as equals. Despite their differences, however, all these writers would agree with Curle that a true education must liberate people from enslavement to a system which values service to human greed for power and possession above the development of awareness and empathy.

Such a transformation is crucial if education is to play its full part in the survival of the human race in the nuclear age. In recent years no one has written more persuasively on education for peace than Johan Galtung. It is impossible here to do justice to the full range of Galtung's ideas contained in five large Volumes of *Essays in Peace Research*. In Volume 3 of the essays he is concerned with the

problems of peace inside societies. Here Galtung spells out
different models of society and the educational structure
appropriate to each. Education is politics, 'for they are both
about how society is and how society should be' (1978,
p.347).

Galtung presents three models of society, conservative,
liberal and radical. The first two of these are both in-
egalitarian, vertical in structure, with the conservative society being feudal, aristocratic and caste-based while the liberal society is class and achievement oriented. The radical
society, on the other hand, is egalitarian and community
oriented in which individuals participate in a direct democracy. It has what Galtung calls a revolutionary educational
structure with open access, communal control and knowledge developed through shared participation and discussion.
Moreover, writes Galtung, knowledge in this type of society
is the ability to change things, hence the goal is practice. It
is very similar to Freire's vision of society.

The radical society is basically collectivist with emphasis
on the groups rather than the individual. Galtung, however,
puts forward the possibility of a fourth social structure, a
post-revolutionary society, in which the social relationships
would be egalitarian as in the third model, but at the same
time individualist. The basic goal of this society is self-
realisation, but not at the expense of anyone else. Galtung
does not spell out the details of such a society but it would
undoubtedly be one in which participation would be more
egalitarian than other models, and in which people would
have a more varied experience within the society with a
greater degree of choice in role and career.

One thing is certain though: such a society, like all
others, would be by no means free of conflict. The notion of
conflict as a way of life appears to be central to Galtung's
thought. Most cultures, and certainly Western culture, have
a negative view of conflict. In our religions salvation is
usually identified with a state of rest in which conflicts
have been resolved. In politics conflicts are to be abolished
either by neutralising or eliminating the opponents or by
working them into the system by means of compromise.
Galtung, however, argues in favour of a positive view of

conflict as a challenge both intellectually and emotionally to all those involved. Conflict, he writes,

can be seen basically as one of the major motivating forces in our existence, as both a cause, a concomitant and a consequence of change, as an element as necessary to social life as air to human life. (ibid, p.490).

Galtung's view of conflict owes much to Gandhi. Like the great Indian leader, he believes that the two parties in a conflict ought not to be separated: in fact it is their incompatibility which they have in common and they should consequently strive to arrive together at a solution. This presupposes, of course, a community in which there is contact, in which disputes are settled by positive acts between equals rather than from above, usually by force. Societies with a high level of social inequality and injustice are inherently violent societies for which Galtung coins the term 'structural violence' (1974, pp.177-81). A good example of the way in which inequalities inhibit discussion and understanding can be seen in the Buberian 'learning groups' described by Gordon and Demarest. These attempted to bring Israeli Jews, Israeli Arabs and Egyptians together in dialogue, along lines laid down by Buber, in an attempt to reach mutual understanding between the participants. However, this dialogue was approached in the firm belief that Israel should be a Jewish state and not a Palestinian or secular state where Jews and Arabs live together, a state in which Arab citizens will continue to be a minority whose national aspirations will not be realised. Criticising the project, Hassan writes (1982, pp.226-231):

One of the basic questions that haunts a number of sensitive Jews and Arabs in the project is: If the inequality in status between Jew and Arab in the larger Israeli society is to remain unchanged, what then is the purpose of teaching Jews and Arabs in the project the art of relating to each other as if they were equal?

This situation is repeated round the world by the way in which structural violence very quickly becomes direct violence when individuals are deprived of their potential for self-expression. As Galtung has written, peace is not only the absence of direct violence and structural violence, but the presence of a non-violent type of egalitarian, non-exploitative and non-suppressive co-operation between units, nations as well as individuals, that do not have to be similar. (1974, p.178)

Conclusion

The writers who have been discussed in this chapter have many points of difference between them. Nevertheless, certain basic principles emerge from their writings leading towards a definition of community and its educational implications.

A central theme of this chapter is the crucial importance in any community of equality between its members. Any society in which there is hierarchical division of class, caste, race or sex is inherently a violent one.

Equality however does not mean sameness. Individual differences must be respected. This means not only differences between people within the group, but also the maintenance and preservation of local minority cultures and values. The goal here is equality in diversity and uniqueness.

There must also be means of open communication between the members of the group. Conflicts within groups or between groups cannot be resolved satisfactorily if people are not prepared seriously to discuss their differences. Again, this discussion must proceed on a basis of equality and not rank. Orders from above usually merely suppress problems rather than solve them.

The role of education within such an ideal of community is to develop individual self-understanding within the group. Peaceful relationships can be engendered through an emphasis on individual self-fulfilment, within a community in which the emphasis is placed on co-operative activities rather than indivdualistic competition.

To return finally to Herbert Read, whose ideas in many ways are at the centre of this book. Writing of the changes needed as groundwork for a new, peaceful affirmative civilisation, he says (1970, p.231):

But it is unlikely that these deep, subtle and intimate changes can be brought about by secretariats and committees, by international conferences and polyglot organisations. They will be born in solitude, in meditation; in the family circle and in the nursery school; in the field and in the factory; in the face of specific problems and by conscious discipline; in creative community and in communal creations; in drama and in the building of new cities; in dance and song; in moments of mutual understanding and love. For all these moments and occasions, all that we need ask is peace in our time and an end to the exploitation of man by man.

Part II

SHARED RESPONSIBILITY AND CREATIVE
ACTIVITIES WITH CHILDREN

It is often the case that extremes of behaviour in emotionally disturbed and delinquent children shed light on the working of the so-called normal. And in coming to understand how to remedy what has gone wrong we may uncover much of what is taken for granted when things go right. It is also of significance that a nonviolent (non-punitive) discipline, together with structured caring attitudes, make an impact upon the development of creative powers and of a general state of well-being.

In the course of Part II we shall move from the baby to school-age children and above, and draw from the experience of special schools in which the writer himself worked as headteacher or warden, or came as a systematic visitor over a number of years.

The examples to be quoted all come from severely deprived or disrupted families in England, whose children showed greater propensity than most for destructiveness, uncontrollable anger, resentment and neurotic anxieties which held up their learning.

The stories in chapter 5 illuminate the notion of 'radical society' advanced by Galtung, and quoted by Collinge in chapter 4. They illustrate the working of egalitarianism and shared participation; and also the use that can be made of conflicts when followed by acts of reparation in revealing and understanding underlying motivations.

5. NONVIOLENT METHODS WITH DELINQUENT YOUNG PEOPLE

Planned Environmental Therapy
Shared Responsibility
Reparation
Truth and Suffering
Examples of Shared Responsibility
Teaching and Guidance

1. Planned Environmental Therapy

On the one hand the classic form of psychotherapy with children, as originated and developed from the work of the Freuds and Melanie Klein, takes place in individual sessions. Play and painting are used for cathartic and interpretive purposes and are also held to be important as a means of release from over-rigid controls. Essentially the purpose is to make conscious through transference those old and unconscious attitudes to the real and phantasied parents. Through a process of symbolisation they may be transformed, or their expression may be sublimated.

In these cases the psychotherapist works in isolation from the other adults with whom the child has contact, whether they sympathise with, or are hostile to, what is being done—it is quite possible, for example, for a psychotherapist to hold sessions in a prison or remand home which is by design punitive or custodial, not therapeutic.

On the other hand it is owed to Aichhorn (1925), working in Vienna with his 'aggressive group' in the 1920s, that it was realised that an approach could be made to a child by inducing him or her to form a passionate attachment to the worker or teacher—provided the latter were adequately supported—instead of to the therapist. Aichhorn distinguished his method, which is an application of psychoanalysis outside the formal session, by calling it re-education. The name is apt since education here means bringing up, in the sense that ordinary devoted parents bring up their baby. The task for the therapist is not only to break down and to analyse but also to build up and to synthesise.

There follows an example from Greenways, a special residential boys' school, of the use by a psychotherapist of *environmental therapy*, as distinct from sessional treatment, and linked with what went on in the classroom.

Donald's mother was a prostitute; he was daily in the company of her men and became involved in their quarrels. One afternoon, when he was eleven, his mother returned home and from her almost demented conversation he discovered that she had gone to the river and drowned the baby she had borne a few weeks previously and her comments seemed to suggest that she would kill herself. She left the house and presently he followed what he believed to be her path, to discover, by the side of the river about an hour later, some men and policemen standing over her drowned body on the same part of the river in which earlier that day she had drowned her baby.

He was now put into care of the local children's committee, but his aggressive, truculent and dishonest behaviour caused his quick passage from altogether six Homes, one after another.

Quite obviously the challenge to a child who had no reason to believe in other people's trustworthiness was very deep and if we were to succeed we had to withstand whatever reactive test he inflicted upon us...It is insufficient to be patient; it is insufficient to give affection, but both have a promise of success if the boy is continually told why he is doing the thing that not only hurts others but bars the affection of others and therefore hurts him as well. The path was long but after five months he had begun to smile; he had taken to asking for instead of demanding things, but at no time had any moral advice been offered, as clearly such would be highly suspect.

His first Christmas came and as it was undesirable for him to return to his home area, he was asked if he would like to accept an invitation, if such were offered, from a staff member. He chose and the invitation was forthcoming. Along with this family, Donald had his own pile of presents which included a bicycle. When he had received it on that Christmas morning, so it is reported, a real sense of gratitude glowed.

After this fortnight his return to school was marked by a relapse to his unhappy truculence and it was noticed that he was wearing a watch, the result, it later transpired, of a kind of forced loan. To have asked the obvious question would have denied the trust hitherto shown to him. The therapist took off his own watch before meeting him, seemingly by chance, in the corridor and lifting his wrist called, 'Oh damn, I've left my watch somewhere. Do you know the time Donald?' Two days later on hearing that the watch had been returned to the other boy, the therapist ordered Donald sharply: 'Come to my house at 7.45 tomorrow morning'. Despite protests, he came, had breakfast and was taken to a shop in the village where it had previously been arranged that the most expensive watch stocked should not cost more than three pounds. The therapist then asked him to choose the one he liked and when he had done so said, 'Right. That is yours.' Immediately he demurred, 'Oh, I can't take that, it's too valuable'. A few seconds later he was crying.

Somewhat later, the English teacher reported an inexplicable deterioration in Donald's spelling. Words involving a, e, f, d and r, he could not get right and he brought the matter up in private session. The therapist asked him to write the five offending letters on cards and arrange them in any way his imagination suggested. After some hesitation the word FREDA appeared, at which Donald blushed and began to sob. 'That's my mother's name. She was called Freda' over and over again he muttered. At the same time of the curious impairment of his spelling he had realised it was the second anniversary of his mother's death; the discussion was later shown to have remedied the mis-spelling.

Needless to say, his relationships with adults, and with the boys generally, improved. He left for a university and shortly afterwards was to get married.

Of the many points in this story, it is told to show a potential thief halted, without punishment, and made whole through demonstrated trust and skilful understanding. The therapist commented 'We anticipate theft. It is little good to pardon by some gift what has symbolically been stolen.'

2. Shared Responsibility

A special application of a therapeutically planned environment has been corroborated by Bettelheim (1950) and Redl (1951) in their work with children and by developments of milieu therapy in mental hospitals on both sides of the Atlantic.

Milieu therapy is a situation in which staff and adult patients are integrated into a single, close-knit, self-governing community. In many cases, this means hardly more than a transition from impersonal authority rule to friendly paternalism expressed in a discriminating concern about the patient's feelings and wishes, and a liberal regime. The central feature of milieu therapy, however, is its shared responsibility. The patients meet the doctors and nurses on an equal social footing; and they are encouraged to take collective decisions.

The system of 'self-government' for children at the Ford Republic, USA, in 1908, as a political or democratic sentiment, regarded the practice of egalitarianism as a training in citizenship which would promote selfrespect. This method, exemplified by Homer Lane (Wills, 1964), has been elaborated into a system by which children or young people are not asked to provide their own separate authority but *to share responsibility* with the adults for the welfare of the community.

Usually under such systems the children are incorporated over certain areas into the staff team, whether or not individual psychotherapy, or re-education in Aichhorn's sense, occurs. David Willis (1941, 1945, 1960) advocated shared responsibility as a therapeutic device; not as a particularly effective form of administration, but as a way to enable children to verbalise their problems. He contended that it gives the opportunity for positive effort on the part of the individual and does not allow him or her to evade feelings of guilt, nor to become so lost or submerged in the collective character.

The question of wholeness incidentally was one with which C. G. Jung (1963) was much concerned in his earlier definitions of the process of individuation. He wrote that in general the individual

> is so unconscious that he altogether fails to see his own potentialities for decision. Instead he is constantly and anxiously looking around for external rules and regulations which can guide him in his perplexity... He must know relentlessly how much good he can do, and what crimes he is capable of and must beware of regarding the one as real and the other as illusion. Both are elements within his nature, and both are bound to come to light in him, should he wish—as he ought—to live without self-deception or self-delusion.

To an important extent Wills' contention is based on the fact that the children are not merely simulating or role playing, valuable though that may be at any earlier, and largely cognitive, stage: they are actually dealing with real life problems and the people caught up in them. This offers a deeper initiation into solving conflicts later on.

The most successful work along these lines has nevertheless been marked by a classification of functions. First, what are the areas over which the 'meetings' take responsibility? They may include such matters as stealing, destructiveness or bullying which directly affect the other members of the group themselves; or matters such as wandering, truanting from school or, in a residential establishment, refusing to get up in the morning, none of which inconvenience or impinge upon the others.

There may be some areas such as finance or sickness where it has to be understood that the meeting has not the expertise and must leave decisions to the so-called experts.

Secondly, it is as well to clarify whether the meeting acts in an advisory capacity only; whether it acts legislatively, that is to say makes the rules; and whether judicially, i.e. decides on how to deal with particular cases.

Possible sanctions are of three kinds (Weaver, 1985).
(1) They may be retributive involving corporal punishment, detention or hard physical exercise. (2) They may be consequential such as exclusion from an activity, say swimming, for riotous behaviour; or working to pay off debt for something broken or stolen. (3) What one might call curative such as extra psychotherapy or encouragement to engage in creative activities, or to make reparation.

It is interesting to note that where there is a system of shared responsibility the overwhelming tendency is to favour curative or consequential sanctions, and not to use retributive ones at all. This seems to indicate an insight on the part of the participants into the importance of understanding motivation.

3. Reparation

One way in which a disturbed child's positive attitudes and relationships may be regained, or gained for the first time, years after having passed chronological infancy, is through the reparation of damage and revengeful action.

It may well be that he or she needs to go through a phase of damage—so that other developments may take place. Under controlled conditions, rage and destructiveness may be turned to reparational trends through which feelings of hostility are uncovered, accepted and understood. Thus guilt is assuaged. And aggression, in the intention-to-hurt sense, is atrophied—or sublimated.

Some people regard the shifting of aggression-against-people to the destruction-of-things as an absolute advance, whereas others suggest instead that someone must deal with, and also interpret, the child's aggression. To turn it towards things may be a displacement rather than sublimation, which solves nothing and merely aggravates the situation. If the people concerned under- stand another's need to reject them, to 'annhilate' them, they will feel less wounded or frustrated. Furthermore, if a child can be made to realise that badness is accepted—forgive the sinner but not the sin—this may be the beginning of the withering away of the aggression.

Spontaneous reparative activities have been reported from several special schools, in which the writer worked or visited. For example (Dockar Drysdale, 1953):

Children help with the housework, they wash up, do laundry, distemper walls, paint woodwork, mend holes in plaster, repair beds, light fires, make cups of tea for grown-ups, give parties to other children, comfort and care for small ones, look after animals devotedly, save up and spend money on parcels to send home to their families, make themselves very clean, do jobs of all kinds for people, from whom they have stolen (refusing to be paid), produce abnormally clean and tidy work in class, make bowls of clay, etc., for presents to mothers, grow vegetables which they present to the staff, buy or cook food for grown-ups. The girl who steals may not return the money but she is quite likely to buy a bunch of daffodils and subsequently be able to speak of the theft and speculate as to its cause.

Nevertheless, since much resentment is not overt, subsequent acts of reparation may not be recognised by the staff, or may even be made secretly. Hostile wishes may seem real or effective to the illwishers; children will then make amends among themselves for phantasied damage.

In like manner, real damage or anti-social behaviour may be followed by a symbolic form of reparation. The headmaster of a London day special school tells the tale of a girl who had been particularly obstructive and unco-operative. At the end of the day the staff found the table in their room bedecked with blossom. Nothing was said on either side, but the girl knew that the staff knew she had tried to make amends by doing something for them. This knowledge reduced both her guilt and their suppressed hostility. It is a moot point whether anyone could have improved the situation by verbalising it. The teachers, in this particular case, took the view that the action itself was sufficient; that a movement in the girl's emotions had occurred; that in Koestler's phrase, this had been a bisociative act, linking her consciousness with unconscious feelings. The teachers' function was to maintain an environment in which such movements could take place, interpreted or not; and, indeed, that to verbalise would be to embarrass—though they might have hugged or kissed her.

The partly initiated teacher, or worker, or one who is harassed by conventional requests for orderliness, may be pressed to enforce reparation. As this is tantamount to punishment or duragraha, a shift in tension does not occur. Emotional growth in other words is not necessarily fostered by orderliness or the apparent claims of justice.

4. Truth and Suffering

Some teachers and workers have evolved ways of handling children by nonviolent means that show affinities with techniques for bringing about changes in adults. Satyagraha after all is based on truth and suffering. This includes the principle that symbolic reparation should be made by those who have suffered, or have a grievance, to those who have inflicted it. It is to exemplify the making of atonement and thereby to cause a shift in the tension of emotions and thus perhaps, to reveal a new view of the situation.

In a special school, the long-suffering of the adults can be making up for those who were hostile and lacking in charity in the child's early years; and the offerings of the teachers in the form of knowledge, skills and pleasurable activities, engaged in for their intrinsic interest, can be regarded as acts of reparation to make amends for the raw deals from which the children suffered in the past.

Some schools claim that one of the values of camping is that adults and children share together the discomforts of battling with the elements. It was found at one school that it was customary for a member of staff to accompany a child or a group of boys and girls on a long walk of a dozen miles after they had committed an offence. This could not be described as punishment since the person inflicting it shared it too. But the physical exertion caused a kind of suffering and from this itself a comradeliness grew.

5. Examples of Shared Responsibility

(To indicate the application of caring attitudes and the delicate matter of structuring by the grown-ups.)

Greenways was founded in 1936 as a non-maintained residential secondary school and is for maladjusted boys of above average intelligence.

There is a considerable weight of tradition which gives stability, added to the fact that it is customary to keep a boy on at the school for educational reasons (i.e. not to interfere with examinations for example) even after his technical maladjustment has disappeared.

In the early days the school meeting was run as a kind of enlarged family council, the main object of which was to demonstrate that the adults were not an alien, aggressive and dangerous group, but reasonable and co-operative and prepared to respect the opinions of the pupils. Complaints and accusations (known as charges) were kept out of this meeting and relegated to school courts which were empowered to issue verdicts and penalties.

A later development has been the selection of a sub-group of responsible pupils sitting as a bench of magistrates, hence known as Bench Members, or BMs for short. The BMs have run the courts and acquired prestige in other areas of the school. The precise method of their selection has varied, but each individual must be acceptable to staff, to the other BMs and to the community as a whole. Unlike prefects they have no authority over the other pupils which they can use for personal advantage; in status they more nearly resemble a Scout troop's court of honour.

The school meeting also developed, and has had a number of committees, elected twice annually, which were concerned with Food and Hygiene, Sports, Social Events, Library, Archives, Exterior Maintenance and Decorations. Reports of the committee chairmen are read to the meeting and, after they have been discussed, are rejected or accepted by the community. When this procedure is finished matters raised by individuals which once formed the entire content of the meeting are dealt with. These are now relatively few, for it is difficult to find a subject which does not come into the field of activity of one of the committees.

The committees and the BMs enjoy a high degree of autonomy—higher than would be possible with younger or less intelligent boys—and membership of them involves some practice in public speaking.

Although, from the foregoing description, the system might appear to be predominantly 'political' or administrative, its most important function is contained in the personal relations between adults and pupils. The headmaster (Holland, 1965) explains it thus:

Many maladjusted children are antagonistic to adult dominance, others are suspicious of adults...Difficult parents have set up in the child's mind images which stand in the way of mutual confidence even when the teacher is not made a direct substitute for parents ... But unless such barriers are broken, not only will the staff of the school be unable to give any adequate guidance, but also the insecurity which lies at the roots of the child's maladjustment will be perpetuated. The object of self-government is to place adults in a new and different relationship to pupils which will make it harder for them to be set down, ex hypothesis, as members of a different group with alien aims and intentions.

At *Linscot*, a maintained boarding school for 30 children, aged 7-11, that is to say boys and girls of junior school age, members of staff were organised into teams for out-of-class and weekend duties. The headmaster explained (Case, 1978), 'we don't call our meeting self-government. The meeting is designed to lead to self-discipline and responsibility and of course it has many other facets, such as enabling children to express their ideas. It certainly won't work with any old group of adults as staff...' They found that children need to feel that they are of value to the community. The release that they enjoy when given the opportunity of helping and having some social responsibility is a great antidote to their cynicism. Meetings are in fact held in the first part of each morning and attended by all children and all staff available. The agenda is written out on a large card and is much concerned with arrangements for a great variety of activities. The overall result is one of orderliness. That volunteers for table laying or looking after pets are checked up on by the meeting makes for efficiency.

The headmaster describes the meeting thus:

The central feature of community life is the school meeting. It is eight years old and traditions have been established which make it possible for a child to conduct it. Very few children refuse to do so. The school sits in a circle, with the child chairman sitting at a table at some point in the circle.

The other important office is that of the writer, not of minutes, but of the names of people wishing to speak. These are written on a wall board opposite the chair, thus relieving the chairman of the burden of remembering many names. Herein lies one example of the secret of a well conducted meeting.

Meetings depend for their success on the artistry of the adults responsible, and they must neither dictate, dominate nor withdraw. They must know when the children will proceed to a conclusion without help, must be watchful of the excessive intervention of other staff, and must also know when the children are calling for help, and be able, briefly and unobtrusively, to throw in the remark which goads the meeting into fresh searching.

The chairman has the agreed agenda and this covers the business of daily social living. The meeting opens with some cultural activity, such as a piece of music chosen by the children or staff, a play, a talk or exhibition of work. This is followed by announcements about the arrival of letters, and any other activities occurring during the day.

In question time, children and staff raise their day-to-day problems, but vigorous discussion may take place at any point on the agenda and take up a major part of the meeting.

Children are thus enabled to hear a wide range of opinions at all levels of age and maturation. But here, as everywhere in a school for the maladjusted, there must be a core of experienced children who have come through. Without this there can be no evident goal for the uninitiated. The former are more able to accept that the meeting does not always grant what is required; they are less likely to be moved by hateful or shallow comment, they can indulge in hard hitting comment without fear!

6. Teaching and Guidance

It must be acknowledged that the meetings just described are to some extent stage-managed. This is because the therapeutic task of leadership with young people is to raise the general level of perception, consciousness and intuition. The leader acts as some kind of a prophet from whose clarifications people learn. The essential part of authority in a nonviolent discipline is the capacity for extra loving.

Yet there is a sternness about this which is far removed from possessiveness.

Its two aspects concern teaching and guidance. In *teaching* this covers the vexed question of indoctrination, whether as bias in history or the inculcation of religious or moral values.

A reciprocal relationship surpasses the role of the teacher who pumps knowledge into the pupil, as well as the one who, reacting against this, is in fact merely a purveyor, no matter how temptingly the wares are set out. The teacher sees the situation from both ends, the learner from one only. As soon as the learner appreciates the bilateral nature of the relationship, the situation has become one of friendship: but of this many teachers are afraid.

Ultimately a question to be asked is how far *child-guidance* is offered in order to manipulate and control, and how far it is an adventure in human mutuality. A nonviolent ethic precludes the use of superior knowledge or skill by a psychotherapist to impose a form of behaviour. For if the aim is self-determination, the demand which the relationship in guidance makes is for integrity (Morris, 1955). Of this no-one has a monopoly. It implies love, and a continuously shared responsibility.

6. CREATIVE WORK IN SOME SPECIAL SCHOOLS FOR THE MALADJUSTED

The following accounts, based on research done at Oxford (Weaver, 1968), are concerned with four residential special schools in England and with George Lyward's 'place of leisure' for young men at Finchden.

It is suggested that the claims made for the fusion of motility with erotic potential in the integration of the personslity (Winnicott 1958, p.214) bear great resemblance to those made for the significance and nature of the creative process.

The examples are limited to showing that a work of art may on the one hand embody an idea in some significant form, in which case the production is not mere 'free expression', though even this latter may have the effect of relieving tension for the performer; or, on the other, that powerful sensory phenomena are shaped into ideas. Judgement of what is significant, of course, is not arrived at as a purely conscious appreciation of story content, linear dexterity or whatever.

In either case, in the process of creating, a person can be lost analogously to the ecstasy of religious experience or of falling in love. It is in this condition that he or she is 'real' quite as much as when being angry or aggressive, as some of Freud's women patients tried to explain to him.

Froebel, and others, recognised that through play and through making things a child not only becomes happily absorbed and lost to the world, but gains a satisfaction which establishes his or her identity. Froebel's word was *darstellung* or creative self-expression. To galvanise a child into such activity, the results albeit uninterpreted, is the task of any teacher anyway, the effects of which may be as salutary, though as intermittent, as psycho-therapy.

Some teachers advocate entering into activities with the children which do not appear to have a connection with academic learning, such as free play, outdoor games, painting, drama, woodwork. In explaining that the purpose of this is to help the establishment of personal relationships between pupil and teacher, they repeat that 'the prime function of the teacher is not to teach but to help each child to release...emotional tension'. Thus formal work is regarded as something separate from creative activities, and in some schools separate times in the day are allotted for them.

Other teachers however regard the creative process as inseparable from learning itself, as well as a powerful means of personal integration, and of the formation of a disposition to learn. Amongst the best known pre-first world war advocates were Edward Carpenter (1904)

If one lets thought go...one glides below it into the quiet feeling, the quiet sense of one's own identity with the self of other things—of the universe: and so there comes a sense of absolute repose, a consciousness of immense and universal power, such as completely transforms the world.

And Caldwell Cook (1917) of the Perse School, Cambridge: 'The final appreciation in life and in study is to put oneself into the thing studied and to live there active'. The basis for such a point of view has been put forward by other writers, namely: Koestler (1964); Lowenfeld (1935); Rawson (1965 ch.X, p.167); Read (1943); Tomlinson (1944); Viola (1936 and 1942); and in the Ministry of Education Underwood Report (1955 paras. 208-9).

The following accounts of such work were made on a series of visits to residential special schools: (i) independent, (ii) a group of Rudolf Steiner schools, (iii) maintained and (iv) non-maintained; and (v) they are followed by an appreciation of the work of George Lyward.

(i) Princemead School (Independent Special for boys and girls)

The teacher-in-charge insists that the children need constant and strong perceptual experience in order to restore their shattered feelings. He holds that it is too difficult for them to create straight from imagination, but imagination is needed in order to impress form upon, or draw it out from, the original experience. The essential prerequisite for creative work is that the children should be stimulated, even shocked, by powerful forces and ideas which they assimilate and transform.

He is able to provide this not merely by getting his class to listen to music or to handle materials such as stones, fabrics and the bark of trees, but by using the classroom as a place for the distillation of adventures outside it. These might take the form of night journeys through the neighbouring woods—first in a party following a well-known track, then by degrees each child encouraged to make expeditions in twos or threes, or on their own, by unfamiliar paths. Sensing the fragrance of a pine, sudden rush of a startled rabbit, hoot of owl, tree trunks jet black against a languidly clouding moon, these frightened children lose their fear of darkness; no mean achievement for even those *not* maladjusted.

In the summer holiday this teacher regularly takes twenty boys to camp in France at a site perched on the very edge of the cliffs some ten kilometres east of Le Havre. The strong wind blows through the tents, descent to the beach is by an almost vertical path flanked by a thin rope as handrail. Swimming, searching for shells and seaweeds among the rocks, and making a huge fire of driftwood complete the morning programme. A fortnight thus spent in the presence of danger from the raging sea and perilous cliffs, but in company, seems to dwarf each child's own inward fears and to unite the most isolated and anti-social in battling together against the elements.

Invigorated by sights and sounds and scents of nature it is these direct perceptions that are used in the classroom for a sea-horse fabric design, for a deer dance, for the mimicry of a mole, or as the stuff of poetry—and performed to the parents on Open Day. An example of work done in the 11-13 year old group follows:

Midnight Walk

Dank air filled my nostrils
Stealthily I entered the deep dark musty wood.
Tall sentinels stood towering dramatically over me.
Long weird shapes of twisted fantasy met my gaze.
In the swaying tree, a wide eyed winking owl
    sits and stares at me.
Then like a Banshee he leaves his kingdom in search of
    prey.
Scuffling, hurrying under the dark brown leaves, a mouse,
    plump with the fruits of her winter store,
Retreats to the safety of a storm scarred oak.
Low heavy sounds of the grunting sow Badger, scratching
    the musty leaf mould in search of grubs and other
    wriggly earthy morsels.
Beyond the trickling meandering stream, a sleek slim
    silhouette of a weasel, leaping and darting
    like a salmon to her spawning ground.
The trees have not yet their leaves unfolded.
The low moon casts airy creeping moving shadows.
The clouds sifting and sorting themselves move
    rapidly across the deep purple sky.
Gaining strength now the gentle breeze bends
    the saplings in its wake.
Roosting birds disturbed from feathery slumber,
    half dozed fly off in search of stronger, safer boughs.
The sickly singeing smell of Reynard and Vixen
    halts me in my track. Like a flash, there they go,
    zig-zagging through
    the woodman's freshly sawn log piles.
Dousted smouldering logs, flickering back to life
    by the ever strengthening wind.
Faster now the shadows jump like demons from the deep.
Sizzling, spluttering, belching out smoke as the wet soil
    choked its life away.
The Owl, still singing through the bilious sky, hoots,
    screeches and cries as if hungry
Searches relentlessly for a furry morsel in the
    fertile meadow on the fringe of the mysterious wood.
The Vole, parting each blade of grass with care,
    hurrying this way and that in a desperate effort
    to escape the terror of death.
Irritable and impatient now the owl lines up his prey,
With talons outstretched and a blood curdling screech,
    he plummets down to the ground.

In nearly all cases the work begins as a result of a mood which is first created in movement (Laban) and which draws upon recent perceptual experience. For example, a holly leaf when viewed sideways suggested to one child that it was like the crown of thorns on Jesus' head. Then several children took up the theme and produced portraits of Jesus. In movement the story of the crucifixion was finally set to music by the children taking part. The last piece of work thus stimulated was that of a tapestry with a green holly background by a ten year old.

On another occasion three children had found some flies dying after they had been contaminated with DDT. The children talked about this and likened the flies, death to that of human death should there be a nuclear war. The death of a few flies which the children observed to the end stimulated murals, paintings, designs and three-dimensional sculpture. Once the idea of 'nuclear war' had got hold of them the whole school became involved in the movement production.

Dance and Laban:

Movement, associated with the name of Rudolph Laban, clearly implies an activity not merely physical but involving intellectual, emotional and intuitive aspects of a person. Dance goes beyond the strictly functional (as in gymnastics) to the expressive domain, and engenders an insight into the states of mind and the inner drives and moods of the performer as well as of other members of a group. In any case much is revealed about a person in everyday life by the tiny shadow movements of face and hands, or in the mundane tasks of getting out of bed, washing and dressing.

If we accept that an individual expresses attitudes and intentions through his or her movements, so it is logical to assume that by introducing the person to a more varied range of movements beyond the habitual we can enrich the inner experience. This indeed is the key to an understanding of Modern Educational Dance. Laban himself wrote (1948):

He who can transform impressions from the outside world into a unified physical-mental-spiritual awareness, possesses the gift of dance. It is not possible to learn about the nature of things through intellectual understanding alone, nor through emotional sensibility or physical impressions. It is not nature who cheats us when we find ourselves puzzled when our feeling gives a judgment different from that of our reasoning, and when after an exclusive use of our logical powers our emotional faculties are disturbed. It is the incomplete participation of our being which permits us to get hold of only a fraction of awareness.

Sensitivity, after all, develops through an awareness of others, as discussed (chapter 2) in our consideration of Winnicott. Through dance experience is gained in other spheres too—namely in effort and space. Each of these is important in itself as well as being interdependent and complementary. In examining the sphere of group relationships we recognise that our findings are only a part of the contribution that dance can play in nurturing the creative spirit.

Personal, and to a great extent individualistic, ideas may have to be submerged with those of the rest of the group, or they may present a lead in a movement that would otherwise come to a stand-still. Thus co-operation develops, as the individual learns to know him or herself, and also learns to recognise and appreciate the personality of others.

Actions portrayed in dance occur in real life—meeting, avoiding, reacting—and by playing out phantasies, as in other expressive forms, a child especially is helped to grapple with fears, ambitions and other feelings.

Individual performers will differ in their reactions to the formations and patterns that evolve. And, overall, a simple joined circle, for example, in which everyone pulls away from the centre has a different tenor from the closed spiral shape, although shapes themselves are hardly visualised by those taking part.

Dance is concerned with the ideas and feelings behind actual events. That these matters are tackled intuitively and unconsciously is one of its features. The experience of sharing improvisations, inventions and compositions marks a distinction between group and individual performances.

(ii) **Ruderep** (independent special, Rudolph Steiner)

The doctrine which Steiner claimed to have discovered through his study of Goethe was that the artist does not make a sensory phenomenon out of an idea but shapes the sensory phenomenon into an idea. The artist's work on this view does not open the doors for the spirit to enter everyday life, he releases the spiritual content of physical reality.

In their non-verbal psychotherapy the Rudolf Steiner establishments follow the indications of Steiner in engaging the children in music and movement, painting, craft and certain kinds of handwork.

At Ruderep, for example, wool from the flock of southdown-cross on the farm is dyed with natural substances and woven by the pupils into table-cloths and other articles.

Bread is made from wheat produced and stone-milled at the school, the harvest having grown and ripened without chemical fertilisers or spray. The children take turns in the bakery, under an apprenticeship scheme, and produce enough bread for the school (plus a surplus which is sold in the town), and cakes for birthdays and festive occasions.

The common element in both these crafts lies in seeing the whole process through from beginning to end as well as taking personal responsibility for their share of the work.

Furthermore, the activity is aimed at fostering 'perceptual integration' (Havas, 1960). Steiner and his followers (Carlgren 1964; Edmunds 1962; Harwood 1958; Konig 1958; Schiller 1954; Shepherd 1954; Steffen 1921; Steiner 1954; Weihs 1958) have shown that inaction, lethargy and frustration are a consequence of a child's inability to use one set of perceptions, say derived from the sense of touch, in order to verify those derived from another, say sight. The work of a craftsman has the merit of enabling a person, of whatever intelligence, to co-ordinate his perceptions without the need for abstraction. Similarly, eurythmy, or 'music and movement', as practised by Laban and his followers, induces physical co-ordination, which, as is claimed too for Yogi postures, has mental effects. Much of the character of Steiner schools' art and craft is explained by these considerations. Their paintings show the results of definite teaching in technique and initial restrictions to the primary colours.

(iii) **Lambhurst School** (boys' maintained)

At the time of writing there is no system of shared responsibility and no psychotherapy takes place on the premises; the headmaster was originally an art teacher in an Approved School: hence, maybe, the mixture of authoritarian discipline and encouragement of estate work, gardening and crafts.

The visitor is immediately greeted by an array of flowers, and two showpiece glasshouses home-made by the boys. In the art room wood carving is constantly in progress: it is hard work physically but the initial shape of the stump or branch (the sensory phenomenon, as Steiner would have called it) gives an idea, whereas in sculpture or pottery, it was explained, so much imagination may be demanded at the outset that a boy fails to get started.

Such activities provide ample means for unexamined but beneficial sublimation, which more introspective or idealist workers may tend to underrate in their search for deep motivations. It is argued at Lambhurst that these searches are too often inconclusive and that it is better for a boy to retain his complex, for which he may have found a social use, than to suffer a breakdown from which a robust recovery is by no means certain. Indeed this opinion reminds us of the early Freudians, Reich in particular, who bewailed that their analysis sometimes actually made their patients worse. Their reaction, of course, was to delve deeper still, and to place less reliance on free association.

(iv) **Greenways School** (non-maintained for senior intelligent boys; see also chapter 5)

The classrooms act as a kind of testing ground for progress in psychotherapy as well as being sources of benefit in themselves. Schooling is seen to be not merely a matter of increasing knowledge, or of passing exams, nor even of broadening interest, but of building up better *mental functioning* in ways which affect all aspects of the pupils' future life.

According to the headmaster (Holland, 1965), work deriving mainly from self-expression may flourish almost from the outset, but progress in history or geography, dependent to a greater degree on facts, comes more slowly. Acute difficulty occurs in such subjects as mathematics, especially Euclidian geometry, which demand clear reasoning and in which the knowledge gained must be closely retained since new topics require the use of what has gone before.

Though it is seldom expected that delinquent habits can be eliminated by a direct appeal to reason, yet the implication is rarely drawn that some kind of intellectual malfunctioning may be involved in such behaviour. It is very obvious that a realistic approach to knowledge is not easily acquired by pupils whose anxiety makes them obsessional or unable to concentrate. Thus the teacher of science, for example, is not only concerned with the pupils' insight into scientific method, but is also at grips with their illogical and flighty mode of thinking.

'It has often become more-natural', the headmaster explains, 'to take refuge in self-deceptions and confusion, to develop habits of anticipating all manner of possible contingencies irrespective of their probability, and to seek to evade a problem rather than to face it directly and look for a straightforward answer'.

There is, of course, the danger that emphasis on the 'blunt acceptance of facts' may develop into a defensive armour to the impairment of imaginative qualities.

Hence the art teacher, for example, recognises the cathartic value of work done on a conscious level and encourages this in ingenious ways. But he also finds paintings taking shape that are incomprehensible even to the originator since they derive from the unconscious. The task then is not primarily one of stimulation, as at Princemead, nor of sublimation, but of drawing out the boy's feeling and providing him with a means of communication at an emotional level. The teacher knows when and how to help by demonstrating methods and skills, but the actual problems of expression he leaves for the boy himself to surmount. Not to be given such help will lead to an excess of frustration accentuated by the realisation of possibilities. Yet, too, in asking for help the boy may be expressing his fundamental request for approval; slowly as his work is appreciated, and he himself accepted because of it, his intellectual interests develop so that he begins to want to know about the things that constitute the normal school curriculum.

The result is an educational one which is beyond the reach of a psychiatrist, however accurate his interpretation, so long as he works in isolation.

Nevertheless the policy at Greenways is that the psychotherapist does not interpret *to* the boy the products of the art room (though he and the teacher may do so to each other) for the sake of not introducing inhibition or reticence in the work itself. This would seem to be an all too rare and humble recognition, also of the possibility of bias. It is often the case that members of a psychiatric team have conventional attitudes to 'modern art', that they even regard abstract or surrealist work as a sign of mental disturbance, for example Jung on Picasso's Guernica. Winnicott, of course, was another man of exceptional humility who explains (in *Playing and Reality* ,1971) that with an adult patient he interpreted only to show the limitations of his own understanding. He did not regard what he had to say as final or absolute. He held that the patient had the answers and that it was the analyst's job to try and elicit the problem. We are beginning to see, at least from the examples reported here, the intrinsic value of art work; for through the actual process of it something that was previously unconscious is made conscious, whether interpreted or not.

(v) The Legacy of George Lyward (see Burn, 1964, and *The New Era*, 1974, No.3)

The story of George Lyward's work at Finchden illustrates these last remarks, and comes in some unclassifiable way between the specific descriptions of 'shared responsibility' as a means, amongst other aspects, of strengthening the bonds of community; and on the other hand, of the benefits to be derived from an arena in which the several forms of creative and expressive activities are relied upon, fostered and enjoyed. Finchden was a remarkable demonstration of the recognition of the needs for communion and origination, and the interplay of the one upon the other.

After sixteen years teaching at several independent establishments, mainly in the VI form and as a housemaster at Trinity College, Glenalmond, a boys' public school, Lyward was asked by the psychiatrists Dr Rees and Dr Chrichton-Miller to take care of a handful of the former's adolescent patients at a farmhouse, named Guildables, near Edenbridge in Kent.

Five years later in 1935, he moved across the county to Finchden Manor at Tenterden, and remained there (apart from the period of wartime evacuation) until his death in 1973.

The fact that he himself owned the premises had a far-reaching effect upon his status with regard to the staff, and to the quality of 'hospitality' that he offered to the young men who came to stay, as it were—later sent and paid for by local authorities—with him and his family. He had the courage of his convictions to resist any suggestions that, for the sake of continuity, ownership should ever be transferred to a body of trustees.

It is worth mentioning these administrative matters in order to emphasise that in 1902 local authorities in England had been empowered to provide secondary education, but not until the Act of 1944 were they compelled to do so.

Thus, though opportunities varied, as they still do in different ways, from one part of the country to another, secondary schooling was not provided for all but was available for those who could gain a scholarship to a grammar school or whose parents could afford the fees for an independent or private one. There was no statutory provision for, nor recognition of the condition of, maladjusted pupils.

It is in the context of this period that Finchden as an independent—and some, erroneously, say privileged—institution. must be understood, and the universal and lasting significance of the work there extracted.

Comparisons with A.S. Neill

Thus, in the same milieu, in 1925, after a somewhat shorter apprenticeship, Neill started Summerhill, an independent co-educational boarding school the philosophy of which he publicised through his writing and the continuity of which he took steps to ensure. So, whilst Neill's work gained support and emulation in America, Lyward was prepared to let the still small voice of Finchden speak for itself. Perhaps a fuller recognition of Lyward's work is yet to come although, as far as its location at Finchden Manor is concerned, it ceased soon after his own passing.

If one were to make comparisons: Neill freely acknowledged his debt to Wilhelm Reich and the name of his friend and analyst Homer Lane was never far from his lips. With Lyward one associates the Bible, Shakespeare and the influence of C.G. Jung. But Summerhill was co-educational; Neill's creed that every neurosis is founded on sex repression; and that his educational task, likewise Reich's, was to facilitate the unblocking of sexual energy so that complete surrender and fulfilment was possible. Yet, whatever importance there may have been in this as an educational aim, the advent of the pill and women's increasing economic independence of men seem to have made it less urgent. Lyward had reservations about Neill's ideas of homeostasis as that seemed to imply that humanism could provide the balance, whereas Lyward looked for the synthesising and disarming quality of the spirit, or the 'third', as he called it, which brings tension and ease together.

Despite, or because of, his experience at Emanuel School, Glenalmond and Cambridge, Lyward chose to establish a male community and insisted on 'no pairing' (i.e. deep friendships) between the young men on the principle that this would lead them to become isolated from 'the flow and movement of the community'. This may seem contrary to the aim of becoming capable of surrender into a full relationship. Yet Lyward himself wrote (1938, pp.244-5):

...every person is both male and female and therefore in saying 'we will have both boys and girls in our school' certain schools are over-simplifying the issue...(For) the psychoanalytical view was bound to be that the girls, by their presence alone, touch up the boy's fear of the avenging woman—the witch—'the terrible mother' of Jung. Not that this would matter but for the fact that fear is unconscious and will certainly not come to consciousness within a co-educational environment.

Much later in a letter to W. H. Otter, 15 January 1964, he wrote 'twenty five boys asked to stay here for our Christmas fortnight (two Christmas dinners—one with their girl friends; a party—at which there were more girls than boys—and three dances)'. In answering a visitor's query about how long he kept the boys at Finchden he made a famous reply 'I don't keep the boys here: they keep themselves. How long they stay is largely up to them'. And, curiously, one must presume that their sexual life could not begin until they left.

Planned Environmental Therapy and David Wills

Though Lyward quite consciously and definitely relied on the beneficial effects of 'the flow and movement of the community', in addition to its constituting the atmosphere in which he carried out his individual therapy, yet its nature was never formalised either as self-government (attendance at Saturday night meetings was the one thing Neill insisted on) or as planned environmental therapy, which includes the sophisticated practice of shared responsibility, as worked out (and described) pre-eminently by Dr Marjorie Franklin (1966) and by David Wills.

The work of the latter has provided links and encouragement to that of Barbara Dockar-Drysdale (1968) and of Richard Balbernie (1966) at the Cotswold Community which Wills described in *Spare the Child* (1971). In passing, it is worth noting that no corporal punishment, nor grading system, nor numbering of people, nor orders when to leave, nor sub-culture—against which Balbernie launched an immense struggle upon his arrival at the Cotswold Community—had been fully assumed at Finchden from the beginning. Balbernie acknowledges no direct influence from Lyward 'but I would regard that as a pity, as having missed out on something—those that have given me any help or inspiration have been quite other, and through quite different kinds of contact, mainly Neill I suppose, of those early people' (private letter to A. Weaver, 25 November 1976).

In another letter (21 November 1976), Wills provided an interesting firsthand comment:

Lyward was the original Cat that Walked by Himself. He did it is true belong to various organisations and associations, but my impression is that he allied himself to no particular school of thought or psychological doctrine.

Certainly the way he ran his establishment was unique, and if ever such a place was dependent on one charismatic figure, Finchden Manor was that place (witness the fact that it has now closed). It was very clearly revealed if one visited the place that everything hung upon 'the chief', who ruled it with something like a rod of iron, though inside a very thick fur-lined velvet glove, and the presumption is that the control he exercised over those somewhat unruly elements was based on the distinct and separate relationship he had built up with each one. I never knew him as well as I knew Neill and Shaw, and in fact I only visited Finchden twice—once in (circa) 1937 and again 30 years later.

Except for the outside appearance of the rather nice tudor house, it was hardly recognisable as the same place. In 1937 there were uniformed maids, shining dining tables with silver and glass, though I do not exactly recall seeing a butler in a striped waistcoat. Thirty years later one ate at a bare deal trestle table, everyone who could find one brought a knife and fork in with him and, if he wanted to drink, an old can to drink out of. The white-clad chef with his tall hat (that bit I guess—I never actually saw him) had been replaced by a rota—everybody in the place taking it in turn to cook the dinner. It did strike me forcibly in 1967 that Finchden Manor was much more like Hawkspur Camp in many ways than it had been in 1937—the lack of a manifest outward authoritarian control (tho' it was there alright in the person of George), the complete freedom over non-essentials, the 'inmate participation', not going as far as shared responsibility, and the general ethos of the place. In this sense Finchden had much in common with Planned Environmental Therapy, though no formal relationship, and certainly not consciously derived from P.E.T.

No co-therapist

The first point that Wills' letter serves to highlight is Lyward's insistence on 'no co-therapist', in contrast to the Planned Environmental Therapy group (and others elsewhere, for example, Redl and Wineman *Children who Hate* (1951), who incidentally are willing to accept support themselves from fellow-members of their teams, and who allow their clients to select whichever one of them is competent and temperamentally suited to become their therapists, without interference). The main explanation is that it was left to the staff to find short-term responses to deal with immediate and critical situations but they were aware that they could do nothing which might impinge upon the longer-term therapeutic work which was undertaken by Lyward himself. This implied criticism was answered by Lyward who maintained that he selected his staff in such a way that together they offered a very broad spectrum of interest, experience and expertise without ever including a co-therapist. To have done so, he held, would have been to place at risk the 'unity of approach in the therapy which is the vital key to the whole of the work of Finchden.'

Therapy of work

Wills' second point is the mention of Hawkspur which was a camp for young men, started in Essex in 1936, by Majorie Franklin, as psychiatrist and member of the management committee in London, and himself as warden. Unwittingly or not, it bore resemblance to Makarenko's Gorki Colony, founded in the early 1920s, and anticipated the methods advocated by Henrietta Szold in the Israeli Youth Aliyah Childrens' Villages after 1948. In all these, amongst other things, the therapy of work was demonstrated. At Finchden, the young men undertook not only the cooking and cleaning, but also estate work in the form of renovating buildings for their own use, dredging the pond for swimming, or getting a cricket or soccer pitch ready for a match.

Craft, drama and music

The skills required in cooking and building veered over into pottery and craftsmanship in wood and metal, mobiles and light engineering. Whether 'A Man for All Seasons' (about Sir Thomas More, who had once stayed at Finchden Manor) or a pantomime for the people of Tenterden, the dramatic performances called upon the boys' skills not only as craftsmen, in making scenery and costumes, but also as musicians. The drama offered as always a means of identity and collaboration for the actors and an encouragement to learn about the period in question.

Spontaneity and art as therapy

As a scholar himself Lyward communicated his fascination in things of the mind be it in history, music, words or literature. He was a seeker after truth such as that which only an artist can express, without comment. This facet of the man may explain, as Tolstoy emphasised at his school at Yasnaya Polyana, that conditions for spontaneity are necessary for creative activities to thrive, and that these entailed what Lyward called the 'atmosphere'. On the one hand, although the group processes provided the real medium of therapy they were not trammelled, or killed as works of art, by a planned environment; and on the other hand, work in drama, music and craft provided those very means of integration, of making conscious what was unconscious, and therefore of healing, whether interpreted or not, comparable to the process of psychotherapy.

Since Lyward's death, there has been a growing realisation of the place of art as therapy. Indeed Diana Halliday (1976), a founder member of the British Association of Art Therapists, comments on a remark by psychiatrist Frank Tait—'We must reflect the spontaneity of the child's work in the spontaneity of our approach to it, and develop our concepts with his'—that Tait is talking about the uniqueness of each human being as well as of the self-renewing process of artistic creativity and its healing power.

Tagore and Gandhi

It is historically a small step from Tolstoy's school at Yasnaya Polyana to Santiniketan, the school and university founded by Rabindranath Tagore some eighty miles from Calcutta.

Tagore's insistence that an atmosphere of creativity and of culture is a prerequisite for education and an essential inducement to learning is echoed by Lyward's description of school as a place of leisure (from the Greek 'skole'), and his frequent references to the atmosphere necessary for his work.

Poet that he was, Tagore provided a missing dimension to the educational thought and way of life of the very severe and ascetic Mahatma Gandhi—whom nevertheless he revered and from time to time met. It was none other than Gandhi who amplified Tolstoy's belief in non-resistance-to-evil by his practice of satyagraha, which he described as a soul-force, blending truth and love, as discussed above.

Unlike Gandhi, Lyward was deliberately not a political figure. But the immense authority by which he kept Finchden together, and which explains his charisma—in the sense of a spiritual gift, a grace—derived from a similar soul-force and would seem to contain the 'third dimension' of which he often spoke.

Though capable of anger he did not seek power in itself and was intent to help the young men who came to him to become autonomous—'mature citizens of a democracy'. He did this by demonstrating his love, sometimes sternly, towards them and other people; helping them to become loving too; and combining this, in an almost unique manner, with getting them not merely to understand and face the origins of their problems but to act truthfully with regard to themselves and in their current relationships.

Lyward's own embodiment of love and truth gave him a peculiar power which had continually to be earned through his own pain of growing, but which, devoid of dogmatism, makes it impossible to classify him in a particular school of thought. Many of those observing his work tended to perceive him as an intuitionist, not recognising the solid conceptual foundation on which his approach was based.

Lyward developed his principles over forty years. Some other great men in a community of delinquents have achieved a benign status, but based it initially on some act of violence—Makarenko, for example, in his early days in the new Soviet Union actually went round with a gun until he could rest assured that his message of fear would be passed along the grapevine to newcomers to the Gorki colony. Lyward disarmed his recalcitrant customers through getting them to temper the truth about themselves in the melting fire of love. The means and ends were inextricably moral and therapeutic, whereas the notion of mental health alone, as of physical health, has no moral implications. It is a curious paradox that Lyward was regarded with jealousy by some members of the psychiatric profession as though it were obscene for a schoolmaster to dare to enter their special and esoteric field. Yet the greater ones among them, such as Winnicott and Bowlby, who had taught the post-war generation of social workers the importance of early maternal care and the causes and significance of an affectionless character, freely admitted that Lyward had advanced their concepts. However right they had been in their aetiology, he had given enlightenment about treatment.

New (World) Education Fellowship

Little can Lyward have known that in 1937, at the invitation of the New Zealand and Australian Councils for Educational Research, a team of new educators from different lands, selected by the (then) New Education Fellowship, toured the two countries. On the way home some of them broke their journey to make a three-month tour of India. Laurin Zilliacus, chairman of the NEF, and Pierre Bovet, of Geneva, were among those who attended an All-India Education Conference in Calcutta. There they met leaders of the Indian Nationalist Movement, including Gandhi and Nehru and Tagore. The meeting with Gandhi was of special interest for he expounded the scheme he had outlined in Wardha a month or two before. He advocated a basic education for the Indian masses which would centre round a productive handicraft related to the child's environment, and wished that all learning should be connected with this.

It is little wonder that Lyward, a man of such strength and conviction, allied with deep humility and a strange uncertainty, should be sought after outside the confines of Finchden. He himself found respite through the friends he made as a lecturer, as an examiner and as a stalwart of the English New Education Fellowship. It was in 1929 that the Home and School Council was formed as an off-shoot of the ENEF, and such members as J.B. Annand, Raymond King, Dorothy Mathews, Harold Pratt, Wyatt Rawson and Peggy Volkov served on the committees of both; other members included Ian Suttie, Ishbel McDonald and Lord Allen of Hurtwood.

Lyward found himself at home as a member of the committee of the Council and, in spite of his preoccupations at Finchden, contributed to its work by membership of its publication committee, by articles in its widely disseminated *Advances in Understanding the Child,* and eventually by his editorship for thirteen years of its journal *Home and School.*

Lyward succeeded Crighton Miller as chairman and continued during the difficult years of the war. Gradually the five hundred or so affiliated independent and local authority schools began to fall away, and after the war were superseded by a new movement for area federations of Parent Teacher Associations, leading eventually to a National Federation. In 1953 the diminished Home and School Council was re-absorbed into the English New Education Fellowship and the journal was taken over by *The New Era.*

Through the journal, and in his many talks, Lyward had elaborated on the meaning of the delicate triangular relationship between child, parent and teacher, the breakdown of which he so often witnessed at Finchden. Much that was advocated in Britain immediately before and after the war in this regard has come to pass in many parts of the world forty of fifty years later. The innovations that Lyward was not concerned with have been political, in the moves to influence state planning and to secure much greater participation by parents in the governance of schools.

Part III

THE AESTHETIC BASIS OF MORALITY

7. THE PATH OF ART

Healing Power
The Aesthetic Condition
Dewey and the American Scene

1. Healing Power

The art teacher at Greenways (chapter 6 section iv) has in fact become an art therapist whose insight is corroborated by Edith Kramer (1978), in the United States, who has done a lifetime's work with children in art therapy. She tells the story of a boy, Clyde, who came from a broken home and felt greatly concerned about his family. He made a model of himself which was then fired. Kramer describes his delight when the model came out of the oven and had neither exploded nor disintegrated. She said nothing to Clyde but no doubt she had engineered the situation. Clyde, however, said 'I'm alright, I'm still whole. I can go on in spite of all these problems'. Such a story is a good example of art therapy working without interpretation.

Kramer also points out that the therapeutic experience was brought about without a transference in her relationship. She constantly tried to diminish the importance of transference for in such work it is less crucial than in psychotherapy.

This does not mean that the relationship between art therapist and patient is of no consequence. Quite the reverse. It is, however, a different kind of relationship—a three-cornered one. The artefact itself (a number of people have pointed this out) forms the third element: patient, therapist and object. The patient and therapist relate to each other and both relate to the object. Other people can do so, too.

This is an exciting and fascinating state of affairs. It implies, perhaps first and foremost, that the art therapist is a person; a person with certain highly developed skills and insights, rather than a professional who is a person only incidentally. It is therefore more possible for the art therapist to become a friend of the patient than for the psychotherapist. Friendship, after all, would interfere with the transference relationship, on which the psychotherapist's treatment depends.

The friendship between art therapist and patient can become similar to the final stages in a teacher/pupil relationship (see chapter 5 section 6). Here the teacher will have been aware of the child's predicament, capabilities and wishes, and with these in mind provided materials and devised situations which have helped him or her to attain greater autonomy and symmetry of attitude.

Indeed the processes peculiar to art itself encapsulate a healing power. Such an eventuality is similar in content to Plato's story of the people in the cave, who are led out and become enlightened, having moved from their original environment and ways of thinking. Plato believed that if a person's aesthetic sensibility can be heightened then somehow this will be transferred to ideas about justice or social behaviour.

Nevertheless, we are well aware that there is a problem in transferring knowledge or insight gained in one sphere to another. We have to ask ourselves in what circumstances a heightened aesthetic sensibility will spill over into the moral sphere.

2. The Aesthetic Condition

At this point it may be worth considering the opinions of two Romantic poets, Schiller and Shelley—though neither offers proofs, as poets seldom do.

Friedrich Schiller, chiefly known in Germany as a dramatist, was for a short time professor of History at Jena. He was born in the 1750s, the same decade as Mozart, and published in 1795 his *Letters* (to a Danish prince) *on the Aesthetic Education of Man*. One should perhaps remember that his work appeared in the immediate aftermath of the excesses of the French revolution, and that, in moral theory, Schiller was close to Kant. In his eighteenth-century style he is a difficult and contradictory writer—like Rousseau, his mentor. But the admirable translation and commentary by Reginald Snell (1954) makes him accessible to English readers some two hundred years later.

Schiller seemed to consider that the aesthetic condition, as he called it, is important because it creates a mood which transports a person's spirit, so rendering it possible 'to make of himself what he chooses'. Schiller believed that the aesthetic condition has no significance in itself, but that it can help us to attain a moral awareness. It does not merely bring about a catharsis, although such an experience is involved. Nor does it in itself resolve unconscious conflicts.

He says in this connection:

Insofar as he gives form to matter...he is invulnerable to Nature's influences, for nothing can injure a spirit except what deprives it of freedom and man proves his freedom by his very forming of the formless: Man is superior to every terror of Nature as long as he knows how to give form to it and turn it into his object.

If we can accept Schiller, then perhaps we are beginning to understand the effect that is produced upon us by a work of art or by 'impressing form upon a matter'. Shelley, the son-in-law of Godwin, whose *Political Justice* appeared in 1793 just two years before Schiller's *Letters,* also discusses this liberated condition.

The following is taken from Shelley's *Defence of Poetry* (written about 1812 and published posthumously in 1840):

It is not for want of admirable doctrines that men hate, and despise, and censure and deceive, and subjugate one another. But poetry acts in another and diviner manner. It awakens and enlarges the mind itself. The great secret of morals is love or a going out of our own nature, and an identification of ourselves with the beautiful which exists in thought, action, or person, not our own. A man, to be greatly good, must imagine intensely and comprehensively; he must put himself in the place of another and of many others; the pains and pleasures of his species must become his own. The great instrument of moral good is the imagination; and poetry administers to the effect by acting upon the cause. Poetry enlarges the circumference of the imagination by replenishing it with thoughts of ever new delight...Poetry strengthens the faculty which is the organ of the moral nature of man, in the same manner as exercise strengthens a limb. A poet therefore will do ill to embody his own conceptions of right and wrong, which are usually those of his place and time, in his poetical creations.

Poetry is the record of the best and happiest moments of the
happiest and best minds...It is as it were the interpenetration of a
diviner nature through our own; but its footsteps are like those of a
wind over the sea, which the morning calm erases, and whose
traces remain only, as on the wrinkled sand which paves it...
Could there be a more powerful justification for education
through art? The implication is that to find one's own mode
of expression is all important, and that style must be valid
for each particular person. Forms can be sought in painting
or pottery, dance, craft, drama or writing, each associated
somewhat arbitrarily maybe, with Jung's four categories of
temperamental type, namely sensation, intuition, thinking
and feeling.

3. Dewey and the American Scene

It does seem feasible to suggest, as did Schiller, the moods
and mental conditions that are likely to bring human beings
to the point where they are willing and capable of determining an evolutionary process that might bring about a more
humane world in the conditions of their own time and to
their greater personal and ultimate satisfaction.

Heeding those who scoff at the possibility, or even desir-
ability, of human creative activities we might remind ourselves of Kandinsky's division of people into the broad
categories of creators, performers and what he called atten-
ders, or appreciators, of works of art in any of its forms.

However, there is another form of activity that does not
appear to be considered by Kandinsky which is very near to
creativity, namely discovery. This is to leave aside invention
which is not necessarily artistic, but which in the hazarding
of hypotheses does entail originality and imagination.

The foremost advocate of discovery, or heuristic methods
in education, was John Dewey (not to mention Rousseau
'Keep the child dependent on things only'; or Comenius).
He did not imply that the teacher had no role in leading
children to make interesting discoveries, even determining
which were the most worthwhile ones to make. This might
take place in physics or biology and in social relations, and
in building upon them; as well as in what they might
discover spontaneously, and through their own play. Dewey

(1934) observed that the zest accruing to the discoverer was akin to that of the creator, and that what was discovered tended to be more vividly remembered, if there had been coherence in the activity, than what was learnt passively.

Dewey, like Piaget of course, was predominantly concerned with the processes of thinking, indeed he wrote a book on that subject.

It never fails to surprise the present writer when educators proclaim that they have discovered the validity of discovery methods, though that does nothing to diminish the claims in themselves.

The latest example comes from South India. Here a remarkable lady, Sujatha de Magry, trained as a medical social worker, who has little time for education in its ordinary school sense, had the task of improving the health and hygiene of a group of tribal villagers in the region of Mysore. She set up classes for illiterate women who came with their children from several villages to the hospital that had been established in the forest in their neighbourhood. Her method was to elicit from the women what were the problems over food and cooking, child care and illness that confronted the families. As they told her, gradually she was able to draw from them the means, and give them the confidence, to solve them.

They went back to their villages and returned for more classes. They demanded simple practical books and to learn to read. As the sessions continued, they not only surprised themselves in their ability to come up with answers, but were stimulated to find out more, and could not help noticing, and being excited by the fact, that their fellow villagers began to regard them with new respect.

Activities, whether they be intended for the purpose of learning or the release of so-called 'surplus energy' may or may not entail artistic values. However, there are a number of psychologists such as J. P. Guilford (1967), E. P. Torrance (1963) and others, interested in the relations between creativity and intelligence, who have laid great store on activity. In France the concept of aesthetic education as a development of creativeness has a long-standing tradition in the Freinet school. They believe that activities awaken facets of the personality and so promote 'the art of living'. Liam Hudson (1967) has become famous for his distinction between convergent and divergent thinking, whose elements of inventiveness come near to creativity. Unesco's *Learning to Be* seems to tie in with this strand.

Dewey rose to great heights when he wrote his *Art as Experience*, based on lectures given in memory of William James and delivered at Harvard in 1931. From such heights, which he by no means always scaled (as Bertrand Russell pointed out in his *History of Western Philosophy*), Dewey did take a broad view of the nature of the arts, concerned as he was with sculpture and architecture, and with music and dance. He revealed his opinion that 'form is what emerges whenever experience attains complete development'.

His casual remark that what is form in one context is matter in another, shows him emphasising the interrelationship of these two phenomena and, as we shall see, providing a balanced standpoint from which to view them.

Yet Herbert Read, whose *Education Through Art* (1943) appeared a dozen years later, and whose work is central to the present book, regarded it as one of the curiosities of philosophy that Dewey in *Art as Experience* nowhere established a connection between aesthetics and education. Though he may have implied it, his lack of emphasis has been responsible for much of the superficial and haphazard grasp of the significance of the arts that has been apparent in many places on both sides of the Atlantic in the ensuing fifty years. The essential omission seems to be concerned with the nature of growth.

To some people maturation is held to occur as a result of the unfolding of inherited characteristics, analogous to the opening up of a Japanese paper flower when placed in a bowl of water. Not to deny the importance of heredity, this notion is mechanistic, to say the least. Whereas a more valid explanation of growth would seem to entail an interaction in an aesthetic manner between environment (of people and things) and the hereditary endowment. 'The laws of growth' says Read, seductively (1943, p.228), 'are of harmonious progression, of balanced relationships, of achieved pattern. The application of these laws to inorganic matter is (one aspect of) creative art; their application to the living organism is creative education.'

The omission may also explain the limited success and recognition of a man like A.S. Neill who understood very well the dimension of 'communion' (self-government and sexual freedom); but in his own life and in his writings seemed to give scant attention to visual appearances. This must be said in contrast to Dartington, for example, and despite the work of others at Summerhill such as Robin Bond or developments by followers such as Lucy Francis, founder of Princemead (see chapter 6, section i).

Dewey gave his lectures on art, towards the end of his life, at Harvard. Some forty years later a new school of thought has arisen in the same place. This is epitomised by the Project Zero, originally inspired by the philosopher Nelson Goodman (1968), and carried forward by psychologist David Perkins. Project Zero describes itself as concerned with 'The arts', *human cognition* (my italics) and symbol processing'. In so far as they admit that their main interest is in the nature of perception, their work can be accepted as a thorough and ingenious contribution to the study of this aspect of the arts and education.

In trying to show that the creative act is a form of speeded-up thinking they limit themselves to this particular range of creativity; predominantly, in the case of Goodman, to music which has a strong mathematical base, and hence a system of notation which painting for example has not. Indeed Goodman writes that 'aesthetic experience compensates for lack of contact with the real' or 'art is a poor substitute for reality' without reference to Plato's Theory of Forms nor explaining the phenomena of cubist, surrealist or abstract works. Hence his interest in skills in representational art and, significantly, he makes no mention of Jung. Perkins goes as far as to say that 'the arts share enormous common ground with other forms of learning', and thus reveals himself as disregarding the non-cerebral functions of the personality.

It would seem that Goodman and Perkins are happy to ignore the important distinction made by Victor Lowenfeld

(1959) between haptic and visual types. The former, whether child or adult, is primarily concerned with his own inner world of sensation and feeling, whereas the latter 'starts from his environment', and develops his visual concepts into concrete plastic form. For some reason Project Zero seems to be exclusively concerned with visusl types and 'object form'.

Much of their work might be considered as an extension upon a narrow line from that at the Bauhaus done during the Weimar republic in Germany in the 1920s and early 30s, until suppressed by Hitler. The emphasis on visual literacy is associated with industrial design, the form of machines and utensils—which fascinated in a less straightforward way early surrealist painters such as Picabia—and the use of space in a building or town. Project Zero's interest in geometry is concerned with fostering the ability to solve problems in visual modes. It can be argued that this mental gymnastic is quite as valuable in intellectual training as time-honoured translations into Latin.

However, not only does Project Zero appear to disregard the haptic type, but it ignores the therapeutic value of the impact of form itself. This process has already been referred to in the quotations from Schiller and Shelley. The juxtapositions of point and line, of colour, rhythm and grouping seem to exert profound psychological effects which are health giving in themselves, apart from their value in representation in the means of communication.

It is to Rudolf Arnheim, who has had enormous influence upon the American scene and whose most important work was on visual perception, that Howard Gardner, an early collaborator with Project Zero, dedicates his own book *The Arts and Human Development* (1973). Gardner himself is clearly interested in painting and literature, which cannot be said of all psychologists who write about the arts. He did state, before the project was formed, that 'art has the singular potential for bringing man closer to other men by highlighting their common traits', and that children 'use their drawings not as expression of their perceptual images...but rather as a feeler, a spontaneous reaching out to the external world, at first tentative, but capable of becoming the main factor in the adjustment of the individual to society'.

In a work some seven years later (*Artful Scribbles*, 1980) Gardner could say that 'the greatest works...are distinguished by that organic sense of form...in which the parts truly resonate with, and enhance one another', and that 'our perspective on artistry is cognitive, that is to say, how to produce an effect'.

These quotations relate Gardner to the considerations of Robert Witkin, writing in England, who distinguished between 'impressive object-form' which is what Goodman and Perkins are concerned with, and 'expressive feeling-form' which is dynamic, draws upon the right side of the brain, and has relevance for education and emotional well being.

Gardner seems to have shifted in his emphasis and maybe now is in line with Project Zero orthodoxy.

However, things do not stand still. In the United States a contrary movement is epitomised at the University of Syracuse, and has been built up in the so-called Synaesthetic Department by the sculptor professor Michael F. Andrews. He writes (1980):

The cognitive process, whether in the academic areas or the arts, is a process of training and strengthening the faculties of reasoning in the individual. It allows no opportunity to develop one's emotional abilities, intuition as a form of knowing, or for sensuous import as a mode of experience. Affective education, however, is not to be fragmentally considered in opposition to cognitive education, but as a symbiotic partner in an education that allows for a blending of intellectual and emotional knowledge and understanding.

In another place Andrews explains that synaesthetic education implies caring for the learner's own reactions, ideas, and feelings as a result of direct experience.

8. TRADITIONAL AND INNOVATIVE CULTURE

I see the continual assertion of the imagination as the basis of all
spiritual and material life, I see also that to Christ imagination was
simply a form of love.

Oscar Wilde, *De Profundis*

Art is far and away the most educational thing we have, far more
so than its rivals, philosophy and theology and science.

Iris Murdoch, *The Fire and the Sun*

In England, following upon Witkin (1974), the strongest
influence upon art education has undoubtedly been that of
Malcolm Ross who was in a key position, as Director of the
Schools Council Curriculum Study *Arts and the Adolescent*,
to grapple with the day-to-day problems of arts teachers and
their pupils, (principally in the visual arts, writing, dance
and drama). Associated with the School of Art at Dartington and as a director of the Arts Curriculum Project at the
University of Exeter, he drew together a considerable group
of educationslists from several parts of the country. Together, not only were they eloquent but, caring for their
fellow human beings in Michael Andrews' sense, fully
grasped the inter-relationships between the so-called cognitive and affective domains. Ross says (1980):

Healthy emotional growth is bound up with the quality of a person's expressive life: it is vital that boys and girls acquire the
confidence and the skill to give form to their feelings, since without feelings life is not worth living...Feelings can simply go sour if
they do not find satisfactory forms of release—or they suddenly
break out in violence and frustration.

A great merit of Ross's work is that it is pragmatic and
realistically concerned with *how* to find the means of expression. He echoes Herbert Read and Suzanne Langer in
stressing the importance of expression *per se*. But he does
not explicitly discuss whether participation in artistic rituals or ceremonies, as for example by the Spartans or by
the followers of Islam, increased their determination to

offer themselves in violent combat for a political or religious cause. A major explanation of this is given by Ross's most influential collaborator, Peter Abbs, now at the University of Sussex, who founded and edited *Tract*. In this journal, and in his books, he has given a substantial historical background to the modes of thinking stemming from the seventeenth century in Europe. In particular (1979) he shows that in Descartes' concept of the self as pure mind, 'wholly distinct from the body and even more easily known than the latter', there can be no place for the culture of the feelings or the culture of the senses; and least of all a place for the wholeness of heart and mind running harmoniously together.

Perhaps such placing of Descartes, though Abbs does it elegantly, is commonplace nowadays (Whyte, 1979), but Abbs' great contribution is to describe, and stress the need for, both traditional *and* innovative culture.

Traditional culture, most obviously seen in dance and architectural forms, in whatever part of the world, maintains and reiterates the most 'perfect' and hence enduring features of the past. Such stylised achievements in themselves enable people to relate to their own past whether they be Hindus frequenting their Shiva temples rapturously sculptured twenty-five centuries ago, or modern Soviet man meticulously and beautifully restoring the palaces of St Petersburg, and depicting the life of a Tsar whose regime it was the purpose of the bolshevik revolution to overthrow. One cannot absolutely discard one's past, and indeed it is essential to be aware of it. The rituals of traditional culture also strengthen the bonds of community, and promote solidarity and feelings of brotherhood within the group. This has been most noticeable in religious ceremonies, repetitive or otherwise, and it is perhaps apt to quote an eye-witness's account of a scene in Siena when 'The Virgin' or Maestra, just painted by Duccio, was placed in the duomo on 9 June 1311:

The shops were shut; and the Bishop bade that a goodly and devout company of priests and friars should go in solemn procession accompanied by the signori nove and all the officers of the Commune and all the people: all the most worthy followed close upon the picture according to their degree, with the lights burning in their hands; and then behind them came the women and children with their great devotion. And they accompanied the said picture as far as the duomo, making procession around the Campo as is the custom, all the bells sounding joyously for the devotion of so noble a picture as this. And all that day they offered up prayers, with great alms to the poor, praying God and his Mother, who is our advocate, that He may defend us in His infinite mercy from all adversity and evil, and that He may keep us from the hands of traitors and the enemies of Siena.

However illusory the protection afforded from the hands of their enemies—those enemies from a neighbouring city similarly praying to the self-same Virgin on their own behalf—yet the people of Siena would feel inspired to great devotion to their religion and feel a stronger identity with their fellow citizens.

Successful political movements make use of the power of some aesthetic involvement, even if it be no more than the rhythmic beating of a drum. Unsuccessful ones tend to have lacked such ceremonial rituals.

In modern times it has been no coincidence that the first commissar for Education and Culture in the new Soviet Union, after the October Revolution, was A.V. Lunacharsky (1875-1933) who, together with Krupskaya, Lenin's wife, fostered the appreciation of art and creative activities (1906, 1908, 1921). Irena Wojnar (1978) of Warsaw comments:

it was realised that aesthetic education must combine the tenets of cultural and educational policy: that art...must have an effect on the conscience as well as on material reality and that contact with an artistic heritage must be allied to free creative activities. The purifying role of art was also emphasised, as illustrated by remarkable experiments carried out on the public at large, and above all through the theatre.

A state's reliance on the binding power of music and dance is very marked in eastern Europe at the present time. Unless one recognises the impact of ceremonies and rituals it is impossible to explain how present-day atheist Marxists, in Bulgaria for example, can throng to the cathedrals for the celebration of Easter, or other *Christian* festivals. 'Some to the church repair, not for the doctrine but the music there', wrote Alexander Pope, getting but half the point.

Tolstoy, some hundred years later, remarked how hostile people are moved to 'union and mutual love' by hearing a story together, or a dramatic performance or especially music. Indeed his *Kreutzer Sonata* is a terrible warning in this regard. Tolstoy (1898) held that art can promote any kind of feeling. Though he is criticised for moralistic, or didactic attitudes in seemingly advocating what he considered it was right to promote, his critics should quarrel, if they wish, with his ethics, *not with his theory of art*. For Tolstoy gives his opinion that 'only by art can the influence of art be successfully countered'.

At this point it seems that he had in fact grasped the significance of what Abbs (1979, p.13) describes as innovative culture which is concerned with 'fidelity to individual experience'. Without the spontaneity of the innovators the community, which is held together by traditional rituals, will become coercive and tyrannical. Both forms of art are required and they symbolise man's instinct for origination and communion.

Herbert Read's thesis, brilliantly encapsulated by George Woodcock (1972), is that the practice of art, in all the forms that have been discussed in this book, 'nourishes a spontaneity which, incidentally but not accidentally, constitutes a threat to an authoritarian social regime'.

Illich's and Freire's advocacy of participation, and a brotherhood which includes one's enemies, perhaps represents the major innovative educational movement of the 1970s and 80s. Political dictators, however ignorant in other respects, have an uncanny understanding of where the seeds of subversion may grow, and are rapid in attempts to stifle them.

Perhaps we may say of Plato, as of Tolstoy and Sigmund Freud, that their observations have been seminal, but we do not share their interpretations of them.

In the case of Plato we have to remember his very practical fears and disappointment over the regimes in Syracuse, as well as the implications, for the artist, of his Theory of Forms. In a word, for example, he considered that there is a perfect idea of the form of a chair which only the Gods can contemplate. A carpenter actually makes an approximation to this ideal form, which can be sat upon. All the artist can do is to paint some illusory representation of this approximation. The beholder of the picture is thus at least three removes from reality and, for this reason, the artist's work is not regarded highly by Plato for it distracts people from things more serious.

Being pre-eminently concerned with how people can change their lives so as to become good, he concluded that the best, though perhaps not the only, way was to engage in the dialectic of philosophical discussion, i.e. in talk. In the *Sophist*, dialectic is described as a purgation of the soul by argument, refutation and cross-questioning. Philosophy, on this view, to quote Iris Murdoch (1977, p.21), 'attempts by argument and the meticulous pursuit of truth to detach the soul (defined by Plato elsewhere) from material and egoistic goals and enliven its spiritual faculty, which is intelligent and akin to the good'.

The Forms are ideal because they embody canons of balance and proportion, and these constitute the inherent elements of Beauty. Tolstoy accused the Greeks of confusing beauty with morality because they were weak on morality. In fact Socrates could say (Murdoch, op cit., p11) that 'the power of good has fled away into the nature of the beautiful; for measure and proportion are everywhere connected with beauty and virtue'. Good comes to us in the guise of beauty, and the study of form, in Plato's view, liberates the mind. Thus in a well-known passage (*Republic* 401):

Let our artists rather be those who are gifted to discern the true nature of beauty and grace; then will our youth dwell in a land of health, amid fair sights and sounds, and receive the good in everything; and beauty, the effluence of fair works, shall flow into the eye and ear, like a health giving breeze from a purer region, and insensibly draw the soul from earliest years into likeness and sympathy with the beauty of reason.

One of Tolstoy's main criticisms of Plato's theory was that the definition of what is beautiful is entirely subjective, differing from one individual, or from one epoch, to another. Moreover pleasure, the criterion by which beauty is judged, in its irrational nature also has strong affinities with evil and pain. Art, too, is at home with evil and quick to beautify it.

The conclusion to this part of the argument would seem to be not to fall for the over-simplified notion that somehow the harmonies in nature, depicted through works of art, will spill over into the moral sphere and thus make harmonious the relations between human beings. Rather that, through art, whether as creator, performer or beholder, a person's insight and hence empathy, is augmented, so that he or she is in a better position to act justly, and to judge the actions of others.

Part IV

BUILDING FEASIBLE ALTERNATIVES TO WAR

In the preceding pages we have discussed something of the essential nature and needs of individual persons, in all their complexities, from babyhood, through school and as adults. We hope to have shown that, through the persuasive discipline of certain types of community and through the several arts young people, even delinquents, become socialised and caring, and enhance their insights into the lives of others. Thus human beings are moved to moral action. Compulsions and punishments hardly figure.

In Part IV we take a look at the relevance of these prescriptions for the well-being of the planet as a whole, that is to say in the inter-relationships between members within any one society and between national groups.

This involves examining some of the phenomena of warfare itself and the possibility of strengthening their moral and social equivalents through education for peace.

9. SOME PHENOMENA OF WARFARE AND WAYS OF RESISTING THEM

Poverty and Images of the Future
Psychological Considerations
Scenarios for Defence

In the final decades of the twentieth century the most pressing and interdependent problems are to do with poverty; discrimination; desecration of the environment; and with warfare, and its accoutrements, wherever it may occur.

1. Poverty and Images of the Future

Poverty at first sight might seem to be an economic or geographical phenomenon; but the chief cause of it lies in the hidden violence at the back of exploitation of one group by another. Competitive systems in some circumstances may make for efficiency and promote greater well-being than co-operative ones which show a tendency to stagnate. But fear and greed, ancient human characteristics, promote brutality, it seems, whatever the social system.

In warfare, nuclear, biological and chemical weapons have attained such degrees of 'overkill' and destructiveness that their use, to all intents and purposes, has become suicidal and mad. Less deadly exertions, carried out on the responsibility of an individual, or of unofficial militia, rather than by governments are condemned as criminal. The products, and associated research, of the military industries, have become not only self-propelling within a logic of their own (Kaldor, 1982) but of course detract from other kinds of services and production which human beings need—that is to say exacerbate poverty which fans the fuel of violent outbreaks.

Such extremities however, are remediable, and the very fact that the inhabitants of this globe have reached them may force, as nothing else can, a change in age-old habits, even when still in the pursuit of selfish interests. As Kant pointed out, a nation of devils can act intelligently once it sees the need.

Technically, it is known how to increase food production, through a combination of big business and appropriate technology (Schumacher, 1974), which brings with it a renewal of local life and cultural activities. India now produces enough to feed its teeming millions—an immense achievement. But that there is still starvation, privation, avoidable illness and infant mortality is partly due to mal-distribution of food, and storage problems, which in their turn hinge on the violence within the exploitive structure of society. On the other hand, most governments of the world, with much back-sliding, have accepted the principles of the *Brandt Report,* which, together with its altruism, spells out the mutual interdependence of North and South. In the long run Western politicians and their citizens ignore this interdependence to their perilous economic disadvantage.

Moreover, governmental and non-governmental bodies, such as the United Nations Children's Fund (Unicef) or Oxfam, have understood that the way to help the poorest of the poor is to build up their confidence and social life, so that they themselves are not afraid to take initiatives and to devise means by which to withstand their oppressors. One hopes that in the process they will be so educated that when a modicum of power and prosperity comes to them they will wield it wisely and magnanimously. It is also the case that the staff members of aid agencies, and their well-wishers and supporters, get the satisfaction and living proof that their exertions bring results—which cannot be said of much political activity and agitation.

To the present writer the war problem is the more urgent both because failure to deal with it will be literally catastrophic, and because governments, and the public at large, being locked in outmoded ways of thinking, have hardly begun to grapple with the need for alternative means for settling disputes.

It is a stimulating exercise, which one can set one's friends, to envisage as precisely as possible what conditions in the world—politically, ecologically, militarily—one would hope might have come about within the next fifty years; then to reduce the time scale to say ten years; then to one year; and spell out what actions now might tend to lead towards them. J.D. Bernal (1958) put in marvellous perspective some of the astonishing future developments of the resources of the earth that could come about for the benefit of mankind, once the scourge of war is eliminated. Not everyone will agree with Bernal's Marxist ideology, nor perhaps with his emphasis on mechanised cultivation or use of certain fertilisers. However by the use of more land and of existing crops, better breeding of plants and control of pests, possibilities of plenty could be opened up.

2. Psychological Considerations

(i) Constants and variables
We can learn from studies of the past that conflicts tend to operate in a kind of kaleidoscope in which, however, can be discerned three major strands—namely economic, cultural (including political and religious) and psychological. Explanations of causes are legion. Yet solutions can be found by attending in varying degrees to each of the strands.

It has become commonplace to speak of the global village or of spaceship earth. These notions do imply that, despite their differences, human beings have many needs in common. They are the 'consumer needs' for food, shelter and clothing as well as for a minimum of medical and other services.

The consumer needs, we might say, are economic; and with proper husbandry and control, particularly of population, the resources of the earth can meet them, assuming an equitability of social systems.

The variety of forms of expression in language, in the several arts, in architecture and in customs in food and dress, as well as the range of religious and political doctrines, have of course their historical and geographical determinants, and their variety provides a spice to life.

It has now become axiomatic that human beings must, on the one hand, organise economic affairs for the benefit of all, and on the other hand tolerate differences and varieties of forms of expression and belief. Henderson (1968) describes these two poles as constants and variables.

The determination to overcome the clashes of economic interest, which will undoubtedly continue to occur, and to transcend fundamental cultural conflicts, cannot be expected to be forged without psychological and spiritual insight. 'Since 1945, everything has changed' remarked Einstein 'except our way of thinking'.

(ii) Cult of the virile hero

Simone de Beauvoir (1972 pp.95-97), in an illuminating discussion of nomadic life, proposes that the key to the mystery of why it has come about that men have dominated women is to be found in the ancient division of labour by which men went out to hunt and fish and fight while women performed agricultural and other work at home as well as bearing and rearing children. The significance of this division is that 'superiority has been accorded in humanity not to the sex that brings forth (i.e. gives birth) but to that which kills'. The reason for this is that the human male transcends his situation: he is not engaged in mere repetition—even of Life itself—but 're-models, creates and invents.' It is incidental that killing for so many ages has been a concomitant of the process of change and development. Since the second half of the twentieth century it seems that mankind perforce must change his assumptions in this regard, or well nigh perish altogether.

Meanwhile the legacy of past traditions is perpetuated in the finest literature.

In the Western world generation upon generation has been fed upon Homer's stories in which the noblest aim was to die a glorious death in battle. Indeed Hector is mainly remembered for his death and for his body being dragged round the walls of Troy.

In the ancient Hindu scripture Arjuna is prostrated by his dilemma whether to do his duty to fight as leader of the army, or whether to abstain and thus save himself and his confederates from killing members of their own families amongst the enemy. The received wisdom of Krishna is to announce that he should do his duty, that is to fulfil his dharma, by taking part in the battle. The consequences of the war will not bring an end to the world, and, in the process of fighting, Arjuna will indeed have strengthened the social structure by playing his part in it.

In Europe, medieval notions of chivalry depicted the knight as a swordsman and gallant defender of his lady and her honour. The penitentiary pilgrimages of this period were twice blessed; not only were they acts of atonement, like fasting and flagellation: they also gained for the pilgrim the merit of having stood on holy ground. When the Crusades began at the end of the eleventh century they amounted to pilgrimages (under arms for the sake of their own security) but with the added objective of taking possession, from the 'infidels', of the holy sepulchre. The Crusades may be described as the offensive side of chivalry (Barker, 1929, pp.771-2):

> The knight might thus still indulge the bellicose side of his genius—under the aegis and at the bidding of the Church, and in so doing he would also attain what the spiritual side of his nature ardently sought—a perfect salvation and remission of sins. He might butcher all day, till he waded ankle deep in blood, and then at nightfall kneel, sobbing for very joy, at the altar of the sepulchre.

In more recent times Charles Kingsley, in his defence of the Crimean War as a 'just war against tyrants and oppressors', wrote (from Angell, 1911, p141):

> For the Lord Jesus Christ is not only the prince of peace, He is the prince of war, too. He is the Lord of Hosts, the God of armies, and whoever fights in a just war against tyrants and oppressors is fighting on Christ's side, and Christ is fighting on his side. Christ is his captain and his leader, and he can be in no better service. Be sure of it, for the Bible tells you so.

In the final scenes of Hamlet, or in Macbeth's pursuit of Macduff, Shakespeare upholds as natural a man's willingness to commit 'murder most foul' for what he believes to be a just cause. It was for these sentiments that Tolstoy condemned Shakespeare for emphasising this dark side of man's nature, however true it might be, rather than attempting to foster his fraternal feelings.

These few literary and historical examples, taken from

before the unprecedented scientific developments of the twentieth century, contain strong moral exhortations to defend by violent means what is thought to be right and to attack what is seen to be wrong. Saint George, in the legend, had no hesitation in slaying the dragon: it did not occur to him that he might tame it.

A legacy of this righteous attitude had persisted in two ways up to the present time and, though still unconsciously felt, was most clearly expressed in biological terms in the aftermath of Charles Darwin. The first is a confused notion of the survival of the fittest which erroneously assumes, as Norman Angell pointed out in *The Great Illusion* (original publication 1909), that the struggle is against other beings of the same species rather than a struggle for existence within the environment. Without reliance on Kropotkin's *Mutual Aid* (1902), Angell gives many examples of the evolution in human history of co-operation in place of simple pugnacity, and the prosperity gained from it.

The other deep-seated notion is that virility is a quality uniquely fostered not only by armed combat itself but by the organisation of a nation in arms. Mussolini in the nineteen-twenties echoed the sentiment of Professor Baron Karl Von Stengel, a jurist, who was one of Germany's delegates to the first Hague Peace Conference. In his *Weltstadt und Friedensproblem* he says (Angell, 1911, p137):

War has more often facilitated than hindered progress. Athens and Rome, not only in spite of, but just because of their many wars, rose to the zenith of civilisation. Great states like Germany and Italy are welded into Nationalities only through blood and iron.

Storm purifies the air and destroys the frail trees, leaving the sturdy oaks standing. War is the test of a nation's political, physical and intellectual worth. The State in which there is much that is rotten may vegetate for a while in peace, but in war its weakness is revealed...It is better to spend money on armaments and battleships than luxury, motormania, and other sensual living.

Moltke, the Prussian field marshal, expressed a like view in letter to Bluntschli (Angell, p.138):

A perpetual peace is a dream and not even a beautiful dream. War is one of the elements of order in the world established by God.

The noblest virtues of men are developed therein. Without war the world would degenerate... .

Even the first President Roosevelt of the United States held to a philosophy not very dissimilar (speech at Stationers Hall, 10 June 1910 (quoted by Angell, p.139):

We despise a nation, just as we despise a man, who submits to insult. What is true of a man ought to be true of a nation.

We must play a great part in the world and especially...perform those deeds of blood and valour, which above everything else bring national renown.

By war alone can we acquire those virile qualities necessary to win in the stern strife of actual life.

What apparently began as attributes of essential and creative actions in times long past, gradually assumed the status of moral injunctions, although their transcendental significance had been forgotten and is now outmoded.

Since warfare ceased to be a matter of individiaul combat, but of indiscriminate slaughter of women and children and men of all ages, it has ceased to be justifiable on the old grounds. More than that, the devastation of nuclear war is so disastrously ruinous that any perpetrators of it would lose not only their objectives—and their own lives—but fertile lands in which other people might live fterwards.

(iii) 'The need for an enemy'

How is it that the ancient exhortations still find a hold? One main reason is to be found in the mechanism of the scapegoat, upon which Flugel (1945) wrote eloquently, and which provides an outlet for moralised aggression, which is not only socially approved but even demanded. Insofar as behaviour towards the enemy is concerned, what in other circumstances might be described as the actions of a criminal and psychopathic super-ego, become morally justified. The enemy outside induces people to be co-operative, and indeed to feel free from aggressive wishes, towards members of their own side or group. The enemy as scapegoat serves as an object upon which people can project their own feelings of hatred, shame or dissatisfaction. Jung made a

far-reaching contribution in putting forward the concept of
a shadow which consists of the inferior, inadequate or dark
side of our own characters, which we cannot dispel and
should certainly recognise. Some, such as Gene Sharp, plau-
sibly argue that nonviolent methods can be adopted by
people who are still hung up by the 'need to have an
enemy', that is to say they can keep the enemy but deal
with him nonviolently.

Moreover, as has already been suggested, a personally
satisfactory solution to the need for identification may be
found through 'the path of art', rather than through dependence upon a leader (Chapter 3). Works of art, indeed a
society's culture, enhance a person's awareness of his own
identity, which otherwise may be sought by the individual,
or by a whole nation, in opposition to an enemy. In 1982
there was a retrograde resurgence of primitive, because unconscious, unexamined and insular, feelings in Great
Britain against Argentina in the Falklands war. The
Queen's son, Prince Andrew, received a hero's welcome
upon his return, and he himself admitted that he had never
before experienced such excitement and comradeship as the
combat provided.

William James, however, in 1910, had answered the
claim for this special merit in his essay entitled *The Moral
Equivalent of War*. Is the brave man made brave by war, or
was he brave before without publicity being given to his
qualities? War may certainly provide motives for courage
and unselfishness. But so may floods, famine, pestilence
and poverty.

Of great importance is the question of a possible *functional* equivalent of war, a concept to the development of
which much is owed to Gene Sharp (1973) now at Harvard.
To make use of conflicts as a means for progressing to a
new kind of equilibrium, rather than trying to eliminate or
merely to contain them, was after all the dialectical method,
understood on different levels, by Socrates, by Aquinas in
'baptising Aristotle', by Hegel, Marx and Gandhi.

'I am the enemy you killed, my friend', sang Wilfred
Owen.

3. Scenarios for Defence

Social ecologists have formulated a philosophy, and caring attitudes towards the planet and the creatures which live on it, which provide a humane framework for the astonishing, but primarily organisational, scenarios for material plenty envisaged by a man like Bernal.

Assuming that we can dispel the psychological hang-ups to progress just discussed, let us briefly state what seem to be the four main military and political conceptions about defence, exemplified by official policy of the countries of Europe or by the disparate advocates within them. Each of us may temperamentally choose to favour one or other, or some combination, as the most effective or justifiable. In different circumstances and in different parts of the world the emphasis may need to shift.

(i) Nuclear

The first, retaining the time-honoured habit of warfare, is to make use of the latest weapons that have been invented, either for first strike or in retaliation, but somehow hoping that their very existence will act as an infallible deterrent.

The assumption made by the two superpowers, and their allies in Nato or the Warsaw Pact, however, is that, in the last resort, the 'desertisation' and ensuing radioactive winter would be preferable to giving in to the other side. No alternative seems possible to them. It is not the place here to spell out the meaning and implications of such complete catastrophe, nor to list the variations in full membership of the two alliances such as shown by Romania on the one hand, or France, Greece, Cyprus, Spain and Ireland on the other.

(ii) Conventional forces

The second main conception boggles at the genocidal nature of nuclear and biological weapons and believes that a step by step switch to conventional forces only should be made—and that these are quite destructive enough to act as a deterrent too. Among its advocates in Britain are (at present) Generals for Peace and Disarmament, Just Defence, and many members of CND and of the Liberal and Labour Parties.

(iii) Non-aligned

The third category tries to make their countries neutral, believing that alliances lead to embroilment in other disputes, as well as presenting a target for their adversaries. An essential feature of this policy is that conventional forces should be, and be perceived to be, solely defensive. Such countries maintain no bases or colonies outside their borders, do not permit foreign bases within, nor troop movements across, them. In Europe, the countries in question—Albania, Austria, Finland, Yugoslavia, Malta, Sweden and Switzerland—show many variations in terms of the history of their neutrality; and geographically, whether seagirt or landlocked (like Austria and Switzerland), and in their proximity (like Finland) to one of the superpowers. Economically, Albania has adopted, socialist notions of planning, but belongs to no economic bloc; whereas Switzerland is avowedly capitalist and believes in the free play of market forces. Altogether, the countries exhibit a continuum in degrees of political and industrial decentralisation.

All demand a thorough-going peace-time conscription; and rely upon the famous mix of conventional and non-military (i.e. civilian) defence conducted by local militias, organised like an armed home guard. The rationale of dissuasion is that, though it may be impossible actually to prevent invasion, the costs and risks of disaffection brought to an occupying power would become very great, and act as a deterrent too.

In Norway, in World War II, the combination of civilian resistance, in particular by the teachers and church leaders, with territorial and military efforts supported from overseas, prevented Quisling from setting up a Corporate State on Nazi lines. Outside Europe, the experience of the North

Vietnamese shows that a determined people, whatever we may think of their ideology, can by guerrilla methods resist and defeat the fire-power and poisoning of crops, by one of the superpowers, without in fact threatening retaliation.

Important studies of territorial or in-depth defence were made by Adam Roberts (1976) with particular reference to Sweden, Switzerland and Jugoslavia; by the Palme Commission (1982); by the Alternative Defence Commission (Randle, 1983). Peter Johnson (1985, chapter 7) has designed a case to convince Conservatives and the military of the benefits to Britain of armed neutrality, and includes a survey of the history, present pressures and prosperity of the non-aligned European countries.

(iv) Nonviolent action

The fourth conception would radically alter the nature of government and of the State itself. Its advocates believe that war has become outmoded—that the conventional kind can always escalate to the nuclear variety—and that human beings must therefore once and for all on logical grounds devise alternative means for settling disputes and ensuring security. This means civilian resistance to make a country ungovernable by an invader, preparations for which would act as a strong deterrent too.

It implies an attempt to meet an invader, not with armed force but by sustained non-cooperation. Obvious methods are the strike, boycott and civil disobedience against objectionable practices. Though no historical events are clearcut, or can be exactly repeated, the spectacular emancipation of black people in Alabama, and other states, by the campaigns of Martin Luther King is a story of successful nonviolent action which sets precedents for resisters to an invader or occupying power.

In the continuing crises in Poland, however much inflamed by the opposing interests of Soviet and the Nato powers, the struggle by Solidarity has so far been by nonviolent means, and gives an important reason for the lack of military intervention by East or West.

Combined with civil disobedience, Nonviolent Direct Action (NVDA)—or Satyagraha, as Gandhi described the combination of love, truth and willingness to suffer—exerts a powerful influence upon an opponent, provided that it is based on a thorough training.

The chief exponents of this policy in the West have been Joan Bondurant (1958) who gives a sympathetic and detailed account of the dialectics of Gandhi's campaigns; Stephen King-Hall (1958); Adam Roberts (1969); Gene Sharp (1985); and Johan Galtung (1984) who in this, as in his other writings, presents a masterly survey of a very wide range of considerations.

4. Civil Disobedience in a Democracy

The forms of opposition to the military plans of governments must differ according to the relative degrees of free speech and freedom of assembly—on which Thoreau wrote eloquently in the middle of the nineteenth century.

In the democracies of Western Europe or the United States such opposition in the form of nonviolent direct action can constitute rehearsals or training in opposition to an invader (Weaver, 1963).

10. ECOLOGY AND THE GREEN MOVEMENT
IN ENGLAND

Although the habits of warfare persist, many voices at all levels East and West are heard saying that nuclear weapons have now made it an insane and suicidal way of trying to settle disputes. But, as yet, alternatives are not clear. Disregarding such developments since 1945, people argue that the only way to have stopped Hitler was through world war II; that warfare must still be resorted to as a last resort.

The realisation is dawning, too, that weapons are symptoms; that changed attitudes and assumptions will eliminate their use, as was slavery eliminated in the nineteenth century although the knowledge of how to be a slave owner has not been disinvented, and although the wage system perpetuates some of the worst features of slavery.

The rise of the Green movement encapsulates many trends and has a direct relationship with the Hiroshima bomb, although its antecedents go back at least 500 years. As so often in human affairs, contrary faiths and practices have co-existed alongside each other, and, in some respects, it is a mark of healthy civilisations that they have done so.

With deference to Huizinga (see chapter 3) may we nevertheless take 1492 as a landmark in Europe. The Spanish Conquistadors, and founders of the great families of Italy, were creators themselves and patrons of Renaissance artists; they circumnavigated Africa; they crossed the Atlantic as new merchant adventurers and slavers. With them, and in England too the new gentry, born of sheep farming and plunder of the monasteries, were possessed of the triple technology of gunpowder, the compass and printing. Together they produced some of the greatest achievements of all time in literature, painting, sculpture and architecture yet their lives were endemically violent concerned with subjugation overseas, inter-city rivalry and intrigues at home, and predominantly male-dominated. Much of the heroic glory of these people we must admit was a legacy from Greece, the discovery of whose intellectual and philosophical exploits had inspired the Renaissance. Likewise their greed has forerun the competitive materialism so much deplored in our own day by for example Adam Curle (1973).

Moral protest, however, began as part of the stirrings of Protestant conscience in the sixteenth century. Soon afterwards it was cogently expressed by John Evelyn—whose family fortune incidentally came from the manufacture of gunpowder. As an expert botanist and gardener, he wrote *Fumifugium* (1661) a treatise on the pollution of London's atmosphere, and *Sylva* (1664) on trees and timber. It was in his time that Charles II planted the Mall avenue in London on ecological principles, remodelled St James's Park and opened it to the public.

Stately pleasure domes

This type of picturesque garden was to be followed in the next century at Stourhead (1740) and Rousham in England in contrast to the formal continental parks at Tivoli and Versailles. The middle of the eighteenth century saw the magnificent proliferation and evolution of landscape gardening of which Stowe and Blenheim are fine examples. The philosophy of their sometimes enormously rich owners was defined by Horace Walpole (1780) and by J.J. Rousseau. Alexander Pope had declared that 'all gardening is painting', and indeed William Kent (1685-1748) required his gardeners to work without level or line from pictures of the result intended. The creation of garden features which improved the mind or excited noble sentiments was one of Kent's main aims (Hinde, 1986, p.20). Such delectable gardens, fundamentally influenced by landscape painters such as Poussin and Claude Lorraine, essentially worked upon their beholders (still in Descartes' dualistic vein : separated from what they saw) as a dramatic stage tragedy does upon its audience.

All one earth

In the next century the Russian explorer-geographer and anarchist-communist, Peter Kropotkin (1842-1921), epitomises the shift from mere *views* of landscaping, however edifying, and tending to be restricted to the pleasures of the aristocracy, to a philosophy which not only regards human beings and animals as integral branches of the same nature, but upholds the latter, who rarely make predatory attacks upon members of their own species, in contrast to human beings, one of whose distinguishing features has been internecine fighting.

The massive evidence collected by Kropotkin on his expeditions in Siberia as a young man (see Woodcock and Avakumovic, 1950) enabled him to present, most readably, his conception of *Mutual Aid* (1902). Part of his purpose was to counter the naive interpreters of Darwin's *Descent of Man* (1881) and to defend him against the 'red in tooth and claw' suppositions. After all Darwin had gone to some length *not* to make an arbitrary distinction between animals and humankind and he wrote:

It has, I think, now been shown that man and the higher animals, especially the Primates, have some few instincts in common. All have the same senses, intuitions and sensations—similar passions, affections, and emotions, even the more complex ones such as jealousy, suspicion, emulation, gratitude and magnanimity; they practise deceit and are revengeful; they are sometimes susceptible to ridicule and even have a sense of humour; they feel wonder and curiosity; they possess the same faculties of imitation, attention, deliberation, choice, memory, imagination, the association of ideas and reason, though in very different degrees.

Indeed Kropotkin must be seen as a pivotal figure. On the one hand filled with compassion for the plight of the masses of people, as were the early socialists, he pointed to the danger of authoritarianism inherent in their ideals, as we shall discuss presently. On the other hand the monumental achievement of *Mutual Aid* has provided an unfailing witness for the development of ecology in its concern for the welfare of the planet.

A seemingly unwitting follower of Kropotkin was Sir George Stapleton, the first director of the Welsh Plant Breeding Station, whose seven principles, enunciated toward the end of his life in 1960, show remarkable similarity to his predecessor's. They were:

1. Industrial production should be based as far as possible on renewable resources.

2. Productive industries should be designed on a biological model so that residues and wastes are recycled.

3. The soil must be managed as a living material, prone to sickness and easy to destroy.

4. A high percentage of mixed farming should be legally enforced.

5. Nutrition to be treated as the foundation of health.

6. A balance to be struck between the urban and the rural.

7. Economic arguments should never have priority over ecological arguments.

In the introduction to Stapleton's book *Human Ecology* (published posthumously in 1971) his biographer Robert Waller writes:

The supreme biological law is diversity: without diversity neither nature nor society can survive. Stapleton pointed out that, if we model society on nature, then nature gives us as many examples of co-operation and harmony as of competition: and indeed competition itself has balance and harmony as its aim. Thus it reconciles conflicts that seem to man irreconcilable.

During the ninteenth century, after the establishment of the Linnean Society (1788), for a variety of motives sometimes associated with biological interests stimulated in the regions of the British Empire, a number of professional-scientific, or voluntary but well endowed bodies, proliferated—for example, *Zoological Society* (1826), *Botanical Society* (1836), *Royal Society for the Prevention of Cruelty to Animals* (1824), *Royal Society for the Protection of Birds* (1889), *National Trust* (1895). The present century has brought the *Council for the Protection of Rural England* (1926), *Forestry Commission* (1919), *National Parks Commission, Nature Conservancy Council* (under an Act of 1949) and the *Countryside Commission* (under the Act of 1968).

The late 1960s, coinciding with the period of students' revolts and a greater autonomy in places of learning, saw the founding of journals such as *Resurgence* (1967), and *The Ecologist* (1970), together with bodies like *Friends of the Earth* (1970), *Greenpeace* (1971), and *Turning Point* (1975), all of which continue to be influential in their different ways.

Origins of the Green Movement

In the 1970s there emerged a shifting complex of groups concerned with nuclear power, nuclear waste, saving the whales, chemical warfare, bloodsports, whole food, alternative medicine, feminism, Scots and Welsh nationalism, the Third World. This culminated in a renaissance of the nuclear disarmament movement internationally and on a new scale; and in the Ecology (now Green) Party, following upon the German model, which took off from a network of gatherings, fairs, jazz and rock festivals linked with the hippies and multifarious things alternative of which drug addiction is the dark side.

The Greens, however, are no mere protest group simply and suddenly concerned with the menace of pollution. Politically they go back at least to the philanthropic early socialists such as Robert Owen, Charles Fourier and Ferdinand Lassalle, refreshingly described in Edmund Wilson's *To the Finland Station* (1940). Some of their experiments and small communities were short-lived, undermined either by opposition from without, or fading away (like the early Christians) through the defection of their members—none of which eventualities invalidates the merits of their methods.

The Greens unerringly recount the evil grime of capitalism and the hardships of industrialisation together with its mean philosophy. They inherit the horror of urban ugliness as demonstrated by William Morris, (1969, 1971; and in Thompson, 1955).

A substantial and somewhat traditional story of their immediate ecological concerns has been told by Max Nicholson (1970), outraged by the threat to a sustainable future. Jonathon Porritt (1984) counterbalances these all too true negative aspects in his discussion of the politics of ecology. He warns too, against the authoritarianism embedded in the reckless greed of capitalism and the stultifying coercive collectives that have existed under the name of socialism.

The Way Forward

What are the ways out? Possible answers draw together the following several strands—women, work, decentralisation and demilitarisation.

Women's emancipation

The beginnings of women's political and economic emancipation can be seen in the West in the nineteenth century and in the East and South in the twentieth.

Mary Wollstonecraft may be said to have set the ball rolling in her *A Vindication of the Rights of Woman* (1792, reprinted 1970). In the penultimate chapter she wrote:

The national education of women is of the utmost consequence... yet men are unwilling to place women in situations proper to enable them to acquire sufficient understanding to know how even to nurse their babies. So forcibly does this truth strike me that I would rest the whole tendency of my reasoning upon it.

Though resting her case upon education, including the broad caring dimension, it was a full half century before appreciable changes in the United Kingdom came about in the form of girls' schools, women's colleges at Oxford and Cambridge and the professionalism of women as doctors and nurses.

On the technical level, the vulcanisation of rubber in 1842 made a new form of contraception possible. Thus the Neo-Malthusian League, which had been ceaselessly advocating family planning was massively reinforced by the arrival of Charles Bradlaugh and Annie Besant. They re-published Charles Knowlton's tract *The Fruits of Philos-ophy* which dealt with birth control and had been first published in 1832. Their subsequent prosecution was given enormous publicity, but the birth rate did start to go down though the population increased owing to the parallel fall in the death rate.

The next phase of feminism concerned votes for women. John Stuart Mill in his *Autobiography* (1854) said: that 'every reason which exists for giving the suffrage to any-body, demands that it should not be withheld from women'. His *Subjection of Women* appeared in 1869. A women's suffrage movement had to await the new century. In 1903 Mrs Pankhurst and her daughter Christabel founded the *Women's Social and Political Union*. The story has been told by Raeburn (1973). By 1927 the franchise included women on the same basis as men. Yet, as similarly in other coun-tries of Europe, US, and the English-speaking world, the facts of voting and of women in parliaments, have not brought the changes of attitudes which their advocates had expected.

For a variety of reasons women's liberation emerged as an international movement in the 1960s. Though separate from them, it was inextricably linked with the Black Civil Rights movement, and with the student revolts moved by draft resisters' opposition to the Vietnam war. Juliet Mitch-ell (1971) gave a lucid account in the early stages of this phase which served to articulate the meaning of women's oppression during the ensuing decade. As with some sec-tions of the Black movement, she advocated revolution rath-er than the style of reforms of Martin Luther King. In so doing she seems to have paid scant attention to the power of nonviolence (cf. Freire, discussed in Part I and the women's *peace* movement).

Work and the gift economy
Other profound changes, however, have occurred during this period through work relationships themselves, and through the fact that many more women than before are

financially independent so that responsibilities between parents, whether married or not, are more frequently and effectively shared.

Work itself should certainly be distinguished from paid employment. Some people derive status satisfaction from the amount of money they earn, while ignoring the so-called gift economy whereby, on the one hand, housewives go unpaid, and on the other a greater satisfaction may derive from work that is voluntary and creative. As a result of automation, and in a more equitable world, shorter hours of labour could provide for the needs of everyone—with the blessing of a much greater sphere of leisure. This has immense implications for the family, for life-long education and cultural innovation.

Decentralisation

The converging of electronic and libertarian ideas make possible an economic decentralisation which could only be guessed at by such a man as P.J. Proudhon in the 1850s (reprinted 1923) and which has been brought up to date by Murray Bookchin (1974, 1980, 1982).

Through modern means of transport and of communication people can be in touch with each other, the world over, more easily than in previous centuries. Karl Popper (1945, vol I ch.9, and vol II p.130) is one of those who has pointed to the defects of large-scale planning, whether carried out by men or women, capitalist or socialist, and argued that piecemeal innovations are more likely to be realistically tailored to conditions, present fewer risks to freedom and are more easily rectified when they go wrong.

On the one hand the work of E.F. Schumacher (*Small is Beautiful*, 1974), now almost a cliché, has shown that light engineering, within the financial reaches of the poorest peoples, can provide the intermediate technology that qualitatively augments the productiveness of their labour. Oxfam overseas can bear witness to marvellously successful applications. In the UK they have been efficiently demonstrated since 1974 at the Alternative Technology Centre at Machynlleth in west Wales, in terms of wind, water and solar power, organic food production and the insulation of buildings.

On the other hand, local economic self-sufficiency promotes political independence and autonomy thus magnifying the possibilities of democratic responsibilities. It is the way into a solution of the military defence problem, as suggested in Chapter 9 on nonviolent action. It provides the economic base for deterrence and resistance to an invader in a non-provocative manner.

So we have come full circle. Those who cry for peace and the things that are compatible with it, are joined by those whose primary care is for the planet.

Demilitarisation

Decentralisation, however, is impossible without demilitarisation. Centralised governments thrive on the threats of war: without it political society as it exists today would collapse. The economies and politics of the USA and the USSR are built around the interlocking supply and maintenance of the military industries (Kaldor, 1982).

The German Green Party understood this when it called in its Programme for 1983 for the withdrawal of all troops from foreign territories and for the dissolution of the military blocs, in particular of Nato and the Warsaw Pact.

Given the disappearance of the defence problem, political sovereignty refers only to the area in which taxes are collected and spent. Following a renunciation of war it would be possible to build Europe as a continent of regions extending from the Atlantic to the Urals, working together in a polycentric confederation (curiously enough, without the nationalism this was de Gaulle's plan).

With a Britannic confederation of regions it would then be possible to solve the constitutional problems of Scotland, Wales and Northern Ireland.

11. EDUCATING FOR PEACE

1. What Makes a Man Good?

Theories of education are charged with values about what are desirable qualities in a person; and, rooted in time and place, they reflect current opinions about propositions to be included to meet the demands of future society.

To Aristotle's question 'what makes a man good?' we have, in this book, based our answer on the twin notion of the arts and a supportive community. For the former we drew heavily upon Plato, Schiller, Herbert Read and Abbs. And for the latter, upon Suttie and Winnicott, backed by practical examples of the success and feasibility of a persuasive, non-punitive, discipline even in special schools for anti-social and neurotic children.

Thus we formulated what seem to be desirable contents and processes in which education for peace is merely a specific extension of a more general aim. William Godwin explained that 'the interests of individuals are intertwined with each other'. Stress on character building in the oldest English schools has been in line with this, and so was the prevalence of education for citizenship in the 1930s (Heater, 1984).

In addition to the possibilities, this century, of rapid travel and communication which have made the world shrink, the unleashing, since 1945, of nuclear power opens up hitherto unimaginable prospects for the destruction of the earth, as well as for ways of making it peaceful and prosperous.

It is quite clear to the writer of this book that warfare has become a potentially genocidal way of trying to settle disputes, whether they be economic or ideological or exacerbated by discrimination on grounds of race or belief. This is not to say that disputes and conflicts will not persist, for indeed further endeavours are generated through contradictions. But other ways must be found for solving them.

It is a sign of the times that academics at Oxford are

coming to consider the place of peace studies in education. Yet, sadly, even as enlightened a man as Michael Howard (Kaye, 1987, p.13.) equates conflict with 'the war disease'. How can he be so wide of the mark to assume that in peace studies it is held 'that conflict is something unnecessary, arising from extreme pathological conditions'? Conflict resolution is its very life-blood.

2. Indoctrination

There is nothing wrong in the advocates of peace education devoting their energies to propagating it by the most honest and ingenious campaigns they can muster. But to indoctrinate is wrong in principle, from whatever quarter it comes and in whatever sphere.

What is the answer to this dilemma for a parent or teacher of strong convictions in the political or moral domain? It would seem to lie in the recognition of his of her own convictions. Conscious viewpoint, rather than unconscious bias, in a mentor, can be coped with more easily by the uninitiated. If teachers or parents share the aim to bring up autonomous and self-regulating persons, they will wish to foster enquiring attitudes by various means.

There is however a double edge to this prescription in which 'integrity' or 'exercise in human mutuality' may be the key words. To love, sternly in Lyward's sense, is not to possess, nor wish to control or manipulate, but to help another where he or she cannot manage alone. 'Love and do what thou wilt' cried Aquinas, revealing an inescapable bonding. For as Stephen Coates showed (chapter 3) we tend to adopt, or take on trust, the views and values of those who love us. A mature love, however, permits, in time, a development or complete transcendence which necessitates no rejection of persons. Whereas to go away from an authoritarian mentor entails an overthrow (as in violent social revolutions against an oppressive and undemocratic regime) of ideas and mentor too.

To be specific: a responsible parent, or teacher of very young children, is duty bound to implant certain codes, or modes, of behaviour. Where anything goes, the child is rudderless and cast adrift, without a framework of 'the other' against whom to differentiate. Increasingly, however, and learning from experience, the child can share with those older, and with contemporaries, responsibility for affairs which concern them. This means, as discussed in chapter 5, that morality is discovered through consequences being understood, and through a warmth and sympathy with one's fellows.

3. Peace Education and its Advocates

It is salutary to realise that peace education, as distinct from peace research, is not only interdisciplinary, but is becoming increasingly collaborative internationally. Four regions deserve particular mention:

(i) In Scandinavia, as well as work done at the Stockholm International Peace Research Institute, the *Journal of Peace Research* is published by the International Peace Research Institute from Oslo.

(ii) In the United States, there is a multiplicity of efforts at school and college level provided officially and by bodies such as the Quakers around Philadelphia. Exerting most impact upon Europe in the past decade have been the activities (and funding) of Unicef and other specialised agencies of the United Nations; the Education Faculty at Wayne State University (formerly Prof. Ted Rice); the Institute for World Order (Betty Reardon); and the Peace Studies Programme at Colgate University, Hamilton, New York (Prof. Nigel Young).

(iii) In Australia a proliferation of courses at university and college level, surveyed by Heather Neilson (see *PEP Talk* No.8, 1985).

(iv) In India the work of the Gandhi Foundation in Delhi and elsewhere, and the recently set up courses in peace education at the university at Ahmadabad (Prof. Pathak).

In addition, in Great Britain, to which at the moment we shall devote the greatest space, there are many approaches to the field of peace studies. The most all embracing and one of the most recent (at first hardly more than to do with immigrants' language difficulties) has been Multicultural Education which has made a substantial 'community input' (Lashley, 1983) at a variety of social and political levels.

The title 'peace studies' is suspect in some quarters as representing an unrealistic and unwanted pacifist pipedream. Advocates point out that one does not have to be a pacifist to be nonviolent, but they feel they should make no bones of what they are about.

For those unfamiliar with the field of education for peace it is worth recounting the outstanding work of Robin Richardson who developed the World Studies Project started by James Henderson in the early 1970s, and whose Bulletin was incorporated into *The New Era*, journal of the World Education Fellowship. Richardson eventually moved, appropriately enough, to become adviser on Multicultural Education for the County of Berkshire. The Project, which later pioneered emphasis on 8-13 year olds, has been immensely enriched by David Hicks through whose efforts was established the Centre for Peace Studies at St Martin's College, Lancaster.

These three persons have been prolific in their writings and influential among teachers. They have been closely associated in outlook with the international Sixth Form Atlantic College in South Wales (Colin Reid); the Centre for Global Education at the University of York (David Selby); the Council for Education in World Citizenship (Margaret Quass); the Education Department of Oxfam; and the Centre for World Development Education.

At different stages, mostly in the present decade, have sprung up a profusion of other educational bodies all rejecting the use or possession of nuclear weapons, some rejecting warfare altogether, including, Quaker Peace and Service; Pax Christi (Roman Catholic); Peace Education Network, deriving from Atlantic College; and the Peace Education Project of the Peace Pledge Union. All these, and CND's Teachers for Peace, are listed by John Marks (1984).

In addition one must mention that a number of local education authorities have led the way, through their joint political party committees, in providing teacher support-groups and material for schools on the world studies and multicultural models. In particular may be cited Avon, Belfast, Berkshire, Inner London, Manchester, Newcastle and Sheffield. And to this must be added the National Union of Teachers' most welcome concern with these non-salary matters.

Despite a degree of overlapping it is no doubt healthy that such a profusion of activity should be taking place. The various bodies mentioned have their different origins, and place the weight of their emphasis on different subject topics—whether to do with their concern about the perils of nuclear weapons or the injustices of Third World poverty, and whether they 'see Green' in explaining and advocating solutions to these problems.

Derek Heater, in a comprehensive survey of peace studies and of the CEWC in particular (1984), has illuminatingly analysed these bodies in terms of what they are against rather than for, and accompanied it with a 'halo of related subject-matter...which brings each approach into close relation with the others'. With acknowledgements his analysis is reproduced below.

Particular approach	Focus of concern	'Halo' of related subject-matter
World studies	Parochialism	Systematic inter-connections; economic and environmental conditions; other peoples.
Education for world citizenship and Education for international understanding	Nationalism	International conflict and cooperation; other peoples.
Peace studies	Violence	War; armaments; injustice; human rights.
Third world and development studies	Poverty	Interdependence; resources; injustice.
Multicultural studies	Racialism	Conflict; poverty; in-

		justice.
Human rights	Injustice	Racialism; poverty.
Environmental studies	Environmental degradation	Interdependence; poverty.

4. Peace Education as a Field of Knowledge

In fact it has been no great innovation to take the step from concerns of the 1930s with local citizenship to the realm of global affairs, and to try to promote the skills and qualities likely to solve them. The modern teacher is terrestrial in outlook, not primarily loyal to his or her nation, whether American, British, Chinese, Egyptian, Indian, Italian, Russian or whatever. Emotionally we have the precedent, two thousand years ago, of citizens of Carthage feeling that they were naturally citizens of Rome, without a national loyalty intervening.

Yet it is a curious fact that though there are professors of War Studies (for example, at Kings College London) the professor of Peace Studies at the University of Bradford comes under attack even though he is not concerned with child education. It is said that there is no such thing as peace studies (Cox, 1984; Scruton, 1985; and John Marks, 1984) because they comprise no clear definition of content nor distinctive method of enquiry (or truth criteria). As for content, the same might be said of the well-established Oxford degree in Politics, Philosophy and Economics, known as PPE; or Geography; or Education, which are not 'disciplines' as defined by Paul Hirst (1974), but 'fields of knowledge' to which, in the latter case, Psychology, Philosophy, History and Sociology contribute.

The disciplines can be distinguished as much by their methods as by their content: that is to say, for example, the natural sciences proceed by the hazarding of hypotheses and the testing of them by (repeatable) experiments. One cannot make experiments in history but knowledge is gained by observation—the examination and classification of artefacts and written records.

Education incorporates the disciplines of which it is a part. Peace studies are merely a particular extension. Their content ranges through knowledge of the social institutions of other countries (in the West, for instance, there is a serious lack of knowledge about the Soviet Union, and vice versa); of their heroes and heroines; of the exigencies of human rights; and of the problems of development in third world countries, so-called for being non-aligned.

On the other hand, what might be called education for peace, is directly concerned with the fostering of caring attitudes and, as exemplified in chapter 5, through various types of shared responsibility, actually dealing with the conflicts and social problems with which school and neighbourhood are confronted.

A curious dichotomy sometimes arises here, similar to that discussed in chapter 6, about whether creative activities are necessarily separate from the learning in the academic sphere, or whether they inform and stimulate it.

If we follow Galtung's notion of radical society (see discussion by Collinge, chapter 4), in which the educational structure implies 'open access, communal control and knowledge developed through shared participation', it is easy to envisage the necessary interpenetration of peace education by education for peace. The two hang together no more separately than the two sides of the brain.

Attacks on peace studies are based on three main fears. Firstly, there is an age-old resistance to new knowledge. We remember that sceptics in Galileo's time actually refused to look through his telescope to see the movement of stars upon which his theories about the earth going round the sun were based. In nineteenth-century Oxford Matthew Arnold was one of those struggling to introduce English as a subject against the hold on the ancient universities of the trivium and the quadrivium. What is now known as psychology, was, until the time of William James at Harvard in the 1880s, a branch of philosophy. The study of non-European Egyptian art used to be a branch of archaeology.

Secondly, peace studies not only demand a place in the curriculum, but by their very nature examine the assumptions which uphold the status quo. They include consider-

ation of the concept of national sovereignty, already mentioned; of industrialism and economic growth (Porritt,
1984); questions about alternatives to force and violence in
the ordering of human affairs.

Clear accounts have been given of the content of peace
studies by David Aspin, and of their justification, by Patri-
cia White, in Tubb (1987).

And, as mentioned above, education for peace includes
the practice of shared responsibility in social and academic
affairs, which, perhaps most of all, constitutes a threat to
established habits and ways of learning.

Thirdly, there is a fear that the proponents of peace
studies are soft on the Soviet Union, that willy-nilly their
efforts end in a pacifist unilateralism which is of strategic
advantage to this particular enemy. Enough perhaps has
been said (in chapter 9, parts 2 and 3), to understand this
fear, and to see that the proposed nonviolent action, very
different from Tolstoyan *passive* resistance, is anathema to
a totalitarian regime in which individual personal autonomy is proscribed. One needs to read both Jim Garrison
(1983) on the *Russian Threat*, and Bukovsky (1982).

As peace studies become better formulated and better
practised opposition to them is likely to diminish. Their
complement, education for peace, may soon come to be
hailed the world over as an indispensable extension of the
most necessary patterns in education. From their strong and
gentle streams ways may be found to release the joys inherent in human nature, and to learn 'to form the formless'
from the chaos of modern terrors.

BIBLIOGRAPHY

Abbs, P.	'Education and the Expressive Disciplines' in *Tract*, No.25, 1979.
Abbs, P.	*Autobiography in Education.* Heinemann, 1974.
Adler, A.	*The Neurotic Constitution.* Allen and Unwin, 1921.
Aichhorn, A.	*Wayward Youth.* Imago, 1925.
Angell, N.	*The Great Illusion.* Heinemann, 1911.
Andrews, M.F.	*Sensory Learning.* University of Syracuse, USA, 1980.
Arnheim, R.	*Art and Visual Perception.* Faber, 1956 reprinted 1974.
Balbernie, R.	*Residential Work with Children.* Pergamon, 1966.
Barker, E.	'The Crusades' in *Encyclopaedia Britannica*, Vol.6, pp.771/2, 14th edition, London and New York, 1929.
Beauvoir, S. de	*The Second Sex.* Penguin, 1972 (1949).
Bernal, J.D.	*World Without War.* Routledge and Kegan Paul, 1958.
Bettelheim, B.	*Children of the Dream.* Thames and Hudson, 1969.
Bettelheim, B.	*Love is Not Enough.* Glencoe, USA, 1950.
Bondurant, J.	*The Conquest of Violence: the Gandhian Philosophy of Conflict.* Princeton and OUP, 1958.
Bookchin, M.	*Post-Scarcity Anarchism.* Wildwood House, 1974. See also his *Towards an Ecological Society.* Black Rose Books, Montreal, 1980; and *The Ecology of Freedom.* Cheshire Books, Paolo Alto, California, 1982.
Bovet, L.	*Psychiatric Aspects of Juvenile Delinquency.* World Health Organisation, Geneva, 1957.
Bower, C.A.	'Linguistic Roots of Cultural Invasion in Paulo Freire's Pedagogy', *Teachers College Record*, Vol.84, No.4, 1983.
Bowlby, J.	*Forty Four Juvenile Thieves.* Baillière, Tindall and Cox, 1946.
Bowlby, J.	*Maternal Care and Mental Health.* WHO, 1951.
Bridgeland, M.	*Pioneer Work with Maladjusted Children: a study of the development of therapeutic education.* Staples, 1971.
Buber, M.	'Development of the Creative Powers in the Child', ch. III, Education in *Between*

Man and Man. Fontana, 1961.
Buber, M.   I and Thou. trans. W. Kaufmann, T & T
                           Clark, 1970.
Bukovsky V.   The Peace Movement and the Soviet Union.
                           The Coalition for Peace Through Security,
                           1982.
Burckhardt, J.   The Civilisation of the Renaissance.
                           Phaidon, 1944. (First published in Switzer-
                           land, 1860).
Burn, M.   Mr Lyward's Answer: a Successful Experi-
                           ment in Education. Hamish Hamilton, 1964.
Carlgren, F.   Rudolf Steiner. Goetheanum School of
Trans. J. and S. Rudel   Spiritual Science, Donach, 1964.
Carpenter, E.   The Art of Creation. George Allen, 1904.
Case, H.   Loving Us. Ladywell, Stowmarket, 1978.
Case, H.   'A Therapeutic Discipline for Living', in
                           The New Era, Vol 47, No.7, July/Aug
                           1966.
Centre for Alter-   Visitors' Guide. Machynlleth, Powys,
native Technology   Wales, 1987.
Coates, S.   'Rebels in Christendom', The Listener,
                           Vol.LXVII, No.1731, 31 May 1962.
Cook, E.C.   The Play Way: an essay on educational meth-
                           od. London, 1917.
Crick, B.   'Fraternity: the forgotton value', New Uni-
                           versity Quarterly, Vol.32, No.2, Spring
                           1978.
Curle, A.   Education for Liberation. John Wiley, 1973.
Curle, A.   Educational Strategy for Developing Soci-
                           eties. Tavistock, 1963.
Darwin, C.   The Descent of Man. Republished John
                           Murray, 1981.
Dewey, J.   Art as Experience. (1934) Paragon, 1979.
Dockar-Drysdale, B.   'Some Aspects of Damage and Restitution',
                           Brit. J. Delinq. IV, July 1953.
Dockar-Drysdale, B.   'The Process of Symbolisation observed
                           among emotionally deprived children'. The
                           New Era. XLIV, 8, Sept/Oct 1963.
Dockar-Drysdale, B.   Therapy in Child Care. Longmans, 1968.
Edmunds, L.F.   'The range of Rudolf Steiner's work with
                           children', ch. VI in Rudolf Steiner Educa-
                           tion. 1962.
Education, Ministry of: Report of the Committee on Maladjusted
                           Children. (Underwood Report). HMSO,
                           1955.
Evelyn, J.   Fumifugium, 1661.
Evelyn, J.   Sylva 1664.
Fitzpatrick, S.   Commissariat of Enlightenment: Soviet Or-

	ganisation of Education and the Arts under Lunacharsky, 1919-21. CUP, 1970.
Flugel, J.C.	*Man, Morals & Society.* Duckworth, 1945; Penguin, 1955.
Franklin, M.E.	'The meaning of planned environmental therapy' in *The New Era,* July/August 1966, pp.136-143.
Freire, P.	*Cultural Action for Freedom.* Harvard Educational Review and Penguin, 1977.
Freire, P.	*Pedagogy of the Oppressed.* Penguin, 1978.
Freud, A.	*The Ego and the Mechanisms of Defence.* Hogarth, 1937.
Freud, S.	*The Ego and the Id.* (1927), Hogarth, 1962.
Freud, S.	*Group Psychology and the Analysis of the Ego.* 1940.
Galtung, J.	'Peace Research Takes Sides', *The New Era,* 1974.
Galtung, J.	*Peace and Social Structure: Essays in Peace Research,* Vol.3, Christian Ejlers, Copenhagen, 1978.
Gardner, H.	*The Arts and Human Development.* Wiley, 1973.
Gardner, H.	*Artful Scribbles.* Basic, 1980.
Gardner, H.	*The Significance of Children's Drawings.* Norman, 1980.
Garrison, J.	*The Russian Threat:* Its Myths and Realities. Gateway Books, 1983.
Godwin, W.	*The Enquirer. Reflections on Education, Manners and Literature.* 1797; 2nd ed. 1823, reprinted New York, 1965.
Goodman, N.	*Languages of Art: approach to theory and symbols.* Bobbs-Merrill, 1968.
Gordon, H. and Demarest, J.	'Buberian Learning Groups: The Quest for Responsibility in Education for Peace', *Teachers College Record,* Vol.84, No.1, Fall 1982, pp. 210-225.
Guilford, J.P.	*The Nature of Human Intelligence.* McGraw-Hill, New York, 1967.
Halliday, D.	'Art Therapy in a Child Guidance Clinic' in *Journal of the Association of Workers with Maladjusted Children,* Autumn 1976.
Harwood, A.C.	*The Recovery of Man in Childhood.* Hodder and Stoughton, 1958.
Hassan, R.	'Response to Buberian Learning Groups'. *Teachers College Record,* Vol.84, No.1, Fall 1982.
Havas, F. de	*Perceptual Integration.* International Congress of Psychology, XVI, Bonn, 1960.

Heater, D.   *Peace Through Education* (an account of the
                        CEWC), Taylor and Francis, 1984.
Henderson, J.L.   *Education for World Understanding.* Per-
                        gamon, 1968.
Himmelweit, H.   'Frustration and Aggression' in Pear, T.H.
                        (ed.) *Psychological Aspects of Peace and
                        War.* Hutchinson, 1950.
Hinde, T.   *Capability Brown: The Story of a Master
                        Gardener.* Hutchinson, 1986.
Hinsley, F.H.   *Power and the Pursuit of Peace.* CUP, 1963.
Holland, I.   'The Work of the School', appendix to
                        Shaw, O., *Maladjusted Boys.* Allen and Un-
                        win, 1965.
Hudson, L.   *Contrary Imaginations.* Pelican, 1967. (First
                        published Methuen, 1966).
Huizinga, J.   *The Waning of the Middle Ages.* Arnold,
                        1937. (First published in Dutch, 1919).
Illich, I.   *Tools for Conviviality.* New York, 1973.
Illich, I.   *De-Schooling Society.* Calder and Boyars,
                        1971 (5th edition, 1974).
Illich, I.   *Medical Nemesis: the expropriation of
                        health.* London, 1975.
Illich, I.   *Shadow Work.* Marion Boyars, 1981.
Jackson, L.   *Aggression and its Interpretation.* Methuen,
                        1954.
James, W.   *The Moral Equivalent of War.* USA, 1910;
                        and London, 1911.
Jung, C.G.   *Memories, Dreams, Reflections.* Collins and
                        Routledge & Kegan Paul, 1963.
Johnson, P.   *Neutrality: A Policy for Britain.* Temple
                        Smith, 1985.
Kaye, E. (ed.)   *Peace Studies: The Hard Questions.* Oxford
                        Peace Lectures, 1984-85, Collings, 1987.
Kaldor, M.   *Baroque Arsenal.* Deutsch, 1982.
Kandinsky, V.   *Concerning the Spiritual in Art.* (1914). Hal-
                        liday, Mass., 1955.
Klein, M. and   *Love, Hate and Reparation.*
Riviere, J.   Hogarth, 1937.
Knowlton, C.   *The Fruits of Philosophy,* J. Watson, 1841.
Koestler, A.   *The Act of Creation.* Hutchinson, 1964.
Konig, K.   *The Order of Birth in the Family Constella-
                        tion.* The Cresset, Aberdeen, 1958.
Kramer, E.   *Art Therapy with Children.* Shocken, NY,
                        1978.
Kropotkin, P.   *Fields, Factories and Workshops.* Hutchin-
                        son, 1899. Revised edition Nelson, 1919.
Kropotkin, P.   *Mutual Aid.* 1902. Reprinted, with intro-
                        duction by John Hewetson, Freedom Press,

	1987.
Kropotkin, P.	*The Conquest of Bread.* Chapman and Hall, 1906. Originally published in Paris, 1892.
Kropotkin, P.	*Ethics.* Edited and with introduction by N. Lebedev, 1925; Prism Press, 1978.
Laban, R.	*Modern Educational Dance.* MacDonald and Evans, 3rd edition, 1975.
Laban, R.	*The Dancer's World.* 1948.
Lindholm, S.	*Conjoining Identity Meaning.* University of Stockholm, 1975.
Lowenfeld, M.	*Play in Childhood.* Gollancz, 1935.
Lowenfeld, V.	*The Nature of Creativity.* Routledge and Kegan Paul, 1959.
Lowenfeld, V. and Brittain, W.L.	*Creative and Mental Growth.* Macmillan New York, 1970.
Lunacharksy, A.V.	*On Art and Revolution.* Moscow, 1906.
Lunacharsky, A.V.	*Socialism and Art.* Moscow, 1908.
Lunacharksy, A.V.	*Theatre and Revolution* (and see Fitz-patrick, 1970). Moscow, 1921.
Lyward, G.	in *The New Era.* 1938. Special issue on George Lyward. *The New Era,* Vol.55, No.3, April 1974.
Mackie R. (ed.)	*Literacy and Revolution.* Pluto, 1980.
Makarenko, A.S.	*The Road to Life.* (3 vols.) Foreign Languages Publishing House, Moscow, 1951.
Malinowski, B.	'An Anthropological Analysis of War' in Bradson & Goethal's *War.* Basic Books, NY/London, 1964/68.
Marks, J.	*Peace Studies in our Schools: propaganda for defencelessness.* Women and Families for Defence, 1984.
Mill, J.S.	*Autobiography,* 1834.
Mill, J.S.	*Subjection of Women,* 1869. MIT Press, London, 1970.
Mitchell, J.	*Women's Estate.* Penguin, 1971.
Mitchell, J.	*Psychoanalysis and Feminism.* Lane, 1974.
Mitchison, N.	*The Moral Basis of Politics.* Constable, 1938.
Moloney, J.C.	*Understanding the Japanese Mind.* Philo-sophical Library, NY, 1954.
Morris, B.	'Guidance as a Concept in Educational Psychology', in *Year Book of Education, 1955.* Evans.
Morris, W.	'How Shall We Live Then?' *International Review of Social History* (Amsterdam), Vol.XVI (1971), Part 2.
Morris, W.	'The Depression of Trade', 1885 in *The Unpublished Lectures of William Morris,*

	ed. E.D. Lemire. Wayne State University Press, Detroit, 1969.
Murdoch, I.	*The Fire and the Sun - Why Plato Banished the Artists.* OUP Paperback, 1977.
Nicholson, M.	*The Environmental Revolution.* Hodder and Stoughton, 1970.
Orwell, G.	*Collected Essays, Journalism and Letters,* Vol.4, Secker and Warburg, 1968.
Palme, O. (Convenor)	*Common Security,* Pan Books, 1982.
Plato	*The Laws.* trans. with introduction by T.J. Saunders, Penguin, 1980.
Plato	*The Republic,* trans. with introduction by H.D.P. Lee, Penguin, 1964.
Popper, K.R.	*The Open Society and its Enemies.* Vol.I. Plato. Vol. II Hegel and Marx. RKP, 1945.
Porritt, J.	*Seeing Green: The politics of ecology explained.* Blackwell, 1984. (annotated bibliography pp.241-245).
Proudhon, P-J.	*General Idea of the Revolution in the Nineteenth Century.* Paris, 1851 and Freedom Press, 1923.
Raeburn, A.	*The Militant Suffragettes.* Michael Joseph, 1973.
Randle, M. (Co-ordinator)	*Defence Without the Bomb.* Report of the Alternative Defence Commission, Taylor and Francis, London and New York, 1983.
Rawson, W. and Boyd, W	*The Story of the New Education.* Heinemann, 1965.
Read, H.	*Education through Art.* Faber, 1943.
Read, H.	*The Redemption of the Robot.* Faber, 1970.
Read, H.	*The Cult of Sincerity.* Faber, 1968.
Redl, F. and Wineman, D	*Children Who Hate.* Glencoe, Illinois, 1951.
Roberts, A. (ed.)	*Civilian Resistance as a National Defence.* Pelican, 1969.
Roberts, A. (ed.)	*The Strategy of Civilian Defence.* Faber, 1967.
Ross, M.	*Arts and the Adolescent.* London, 1975.
Ross, M. (ed.)	*The Arts and Personal Growth.* Pergamon, 1980.
Schiller, R.F. trans. Snell, R.	*Letters on the Aesthetic Education of Man,* 1, 5. Routledge, 1954.
Schumacher, E.F.	*Small is Beautiful.* 1973. Abacus, 1974.
Scruton, R.	*Education and Indoctrination.* Sherwood Press, 1985.
Sharp, G.	*Politics of Nonviolent Action,* Parts I, II and III. Porter Sargent, Boston, USA, 1973.
Sharp, G.	*Making Europe Unconquerable.* Taylor and

	Francis, 1985.
Shelley, P.B.	Preface to 'Prometheus Unbound'. *The Poetical Works of Shelley.* Macdonald, 1949.
Stapleton, G.	*Human Ecology.* Charles Knight, 1971.
Steffen, A. trans Harwood, D.	*Rudolf Steiner Lectures to Teachers.* Dornach, 1921.
Steiner, R. trans. Cotterell, M.	*Theosophy.* Anthroposophical Publishing Co., (revised) 1954.
Suttie, I.	*The Origins of Love and Hate.* Routledge, 1935; Penguin, 1963.
Thompson, E.P.	*William Morris.* Pantheon Paperback, New York, 1976. Originally published in England by Merlin Press.
Thoreau, H.D.	*On the Duty of Civil Disobedience,* together with *Walden or Life in the Woods.* New American Library, NY and New English Library, London, 1960 (first published 1849).
Tolstoy, L. trans. Maude, A.	*What is Art?* Bobbs-Merrill, New York, 1960 (first published 1898).
Tomlinson, R.R.	*Children as Artists.* King Penguin, 1944.
Torrance, E.P.	*Education and the Creative Potential.* University of Minnesota Press, 1963.
Tubb, C (ed.)	'Peace Education' in *Cambridge Journal of Education,* Vol.17, No.1, 1987.
Viola, W.	*Child Art and Franz Cizek.* S. Marshall, 1936.
Viola, W.	*Child Art.* (1942) University of London, 1944.
Walpole, H.	*History of the Modern Taste in Gardening,* Strawberry Hill, 1780.
Weaver, A.	'Justification of civil disobedience in a democracy' in *Alternatives to War and Violence.* Ed. Ted Dunn. Clarke, 1963.
Weaver, A.	*The Treatment of Maladjusted Children in England.* D.Phil. thesis, Oxford, 1968.
Weaver, A.	'Shared Responsibility and Reparation' in *The New Era,* Vol. 66, No.2, 1985.
Weihs, T.J.	*The Camphill Rudolf Steiner Schools: for children in need of special care.* The Cresset, Aberdeen, 1962.
Whyte, L.L.	*The Unconscious before Freud.* Friedman, London, 1979.
Wills, D.	*The Hawkspur Experiment.* Allen and Unwin, 1941.
Wills, D.	*The Barns Experiment.* Allen and Unwin,

	1945.
Wills, D.	*Throw Away Thy Rod.* Gollancz, 1960.
Wills, D.	*Homer Lane.* Allen and Unwin, 1964.
Wills, D.	*Spare the Child: the story of an experimental Approved School.* Penguin, 1971.
Wilson, E.	*To the Finland Station.* Secker and Warburg, 1940.
Winnicott, D.W.	*Collected Papers.* Tavistock, 1958.
Winnicott, D.W.	*Playing and Reality.* Tavistock, 1971; Pelican, 1974.
Witkin, R.	*Intelligence of Feeling.* Heinemann, 1974.
Wojnar, I.	'Aesthetic Education' prepared for the international Bureau of Education in *Educational Documentation and Information.* Year 52, No.208, UNESCO, 1978. (Annotated bibliography of 374 titles.)
Wollstonecraft, M.	*A Vindication of the Rights of Woman.* (1792) Gregg Int. Publishers, 1970.
Woodcock, G.	'Herbert Read's Anarchist Masterpiece' in *The New Era,* January, 1972.
Woodcock, G. and Avakumovic, I.	*The Anarchist Prince: a biographical study of Peter Kropotkin.* Boardman, 1950.
Wootton, B.	*Social Science and Social Pathology.* Allen and Unwin, 1959.

NOTES ON AUTHORS

Anthony Weaver M.A. (Cantab), D. Phil.(Oxon) was educated at Stowe school and Jesus College, Cambridge. He later obtained two diplomas from the Institute of Education, London, and his Oxford doctorate is for a thesis on the treatment of maladjusted children.

After teaching in a variety of schools he became warden of a residential clinic for emotionally disturbed and delinquent children. From 1971-80 he was lecturer in education and art therapy at Goldsmiths' College of Art.

He is currently Visiting Fellow at the London Institute of Education and assistant secretary to the Marc Goldstein Memorial Trust for education for international understanding.

Previous publications include *They Steal for Love* (1959), *War Outmoded* (1960); and contributions to *World Questions* (Ed.James Henderson, 1963) and *Alternatives to War and Violence* (Ed. Ted Dunn, 1963). He was editor of *The New Era*, journal of the World Education Fellowship, 1972-82.

Anthony Weaver is married to Alla Perepletnik, a Russian refugee born in Odessa. They now have four grandchildren, to whom this book is dedicated.

James Henderson (1910-1986) lectured on the teaching of history and international affairs at the London Institute of Education for 35 years. He made a unique impact, virtually creating education for international understanding and world studies as we know them, both in the UK and as chairman of the World Education Fellowship.

James Collinge trained as a primary school teacher and graduated from Auckland University, New Zealand. He is now a senior lecturer at Victoria University of Wellington, teaching Philosophy of Education and Comparative Education.